HAYNES MAX POWER Peugeot

306

The definitive guide to **modifying**

by **Richard Nicholls**

HAYNES MAX POWER Peugeot

306

The definitive guide to **modifying**
by **Richard Nicholls**

Haynes Publishing

ISBN 1 85960 909 0

Printed by **J H Haynes & Co Ltd,**
Sparkford, Yeovil, Somerset BA22 7JJ, England.

Tel: 01963 442030 Fax: 01963 440001
Int. tel: +44 1963 442030 Fax: +44 1963 440001
E-mail: sales@haynes-manuals.co.uk
Web site: www.haynes.co.uk

Haynes North America, Inc
861 Lawrence Drive, Newbury Park, California 91320, USA

Editions Haynes S.A.
Tour Aurore IBC - La Défense 2, 18 Place des Reflets,
92975 PARIS LA DEFENSE Cedex, France

Haynes Publishing Nordiska AB
Box 1504, 751 45 UPPSALA, Sweden

It wasn't my idea guv'nor!

1 Advice on safety procedures and precautions is contained throughout this manual, and more specifically on page 186. You are strongly recommended to note these comments, and to pay close attention to any instructions that may be given by the parts supplier.

2 J H Haynes recommends that vehicle modification should only be undertaken by individuals with experience of vehicle mechanics; if you are unsure as to how to go about the modification, advice should be sought from a competent and experienced individual. Any queries regarding modification should be addressed to the product manufacturer concerned, and not to J H Haynes, nor the vehicle manufacturer.

3 The instructions in this manual are followed at the risk of the reader who remains fully and solely responsible for the safety, roadworthiness and legality of his/her vehicle. Thus J H Haynes are giving only non-specific advice in this respect.

4 When modifying a car it is important to bear in mind the legal responsibilities placed on the owners, driver and modifiers of cars, including, but not limited to, the Road Traffic Act 1988. IN PARTICULAR, IT IS AN OFFENCE TO DRIVE ON A PUBLIC ROAD A VEHICLE WHICH IS NOT INSURED OR WHICH DOES NOT COMPLY WITH THE CONSTRUCTION AND USE REGULATIONS, OR WHICH IS DANGEROUS AND MAY CAUSE INJURY TO ANY PERSON, OR WHICH DOES NOT HOLD A CURRENT MOT CERTIFICATE OR DISPLAY A VALID TAX DISC.

5 The safety of any alteration and its compliance with construction and use regulations should be checked before a modified vehicle is sold as it may be an offence to sell a vehicle which is not roadworthy.

6 Any advice provided is correct to the best of our knowledge at the time of publication, but the reader should pay particular attention to any changes of specification to the vehicles, or parts, which can occur without notice.

7 Alterations to vehicles should be disclosed to insurers and licensing authorities, and legal advice taken from the police, vehicle testing centres, or appropriate regulatory bodies.

8 The vehicle has been chosen for this project as it is one of those most widely modified by its owners, and readers should not assume that the vehicle manufacturers have given their approval to the modifications.

9 Neither J H Haynes nor the manufacturers give any warranty as to the safety of a vehicle after alterations, such as those contained in this book, have been made. J H Haynes will not accept liability for any economic loss, damage to property or death and personal injury arising from use of this manual other than in respect of injury or death resulting directly from J H Haynes' negligence.

Contents

Haynes
Max Power

Buyer's guide

Insurance

Suspension

Brakes

Interiors

Security

04

Body styling

05

Lights & bulbs

06

Wheels & tyres

07

11

12

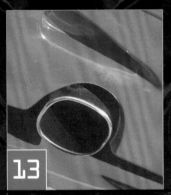

13

14

ICE

Engines

Exhausts

Reference

Haynes Max Power

What's that then?

Haynes Publishing have, for the last forty years, been helping people keep their cars on the roads in countries all over the world by publishing maintenance manuals. Chances are you've either got one of them yourself or you know somebody who has.

"Lights & bulbs" includes fitting high-power blue headlight bulbs, coloured rear light clusters, etc.

Before

After

Remember what it feels like on your birthday, or at Christmas, when you're faced by a pile of pressies? So do we, that gnawing feeling in your gut, what's in them? What did I get? Take that feeling and multiply it by twelve, that's how we felt when we started this project. When we decided that it was time to try something new, we couldn't wait. Because the same theories apply to modifying your car as servicing it, we reckoned we'd better get on and do it ourselves. We don't pay other people to do it for us, and we get the same dodgy instructions with kit as everybody else.

So if you've ever wondered how to fit a door mirror properly, smooth a tailgate or just bolt a seat in, this book is for you.

We've picked up a skip full of tips along the way, and they're all here for you to use. We haven't tried to set any trends, but we've covered every possible process we think you'll need. So where we've tinted a front door window, the same rules apply to a rear one, job done.

If you look in the magazines and want some of that, join us, 'cos so do we, and we'll show you how to get it.

Keeping it real

Modifying a car is not without its problems in the 'real world', as opposed to the seemingly fantasy world of the glossy mags. For instance, it's pretty silly to spend hours fitting illegal window tints or smoked lights if you get pulled the first time you're out

afterwards. Of course, you can get pulled for all sorts of reasons (and just driving a modified car is reason enough sometimes), but keeping the car actually legal is one of the 'hidden' challenges with modifying. Throughout the book, our tips should give all the help you need to at least appear to be on the right side of the law. The annual MOT test is another favourite time for your mods to get panned, and again, we aim to give you all the help necessary to ensure at least that what you've changed doesn't lead to a fail.

Security is another major issue with a tweaked motor, and the perils of insurance cannot be taken lightly, either. We aim to give down-to-earth advice to help you keep the car in the first place, and to help you in not upsetting your insurers too much if the worst happens.

A word about fashion

In producing this book, we're aware that fashions change. What we show being fitted to our car might well be hideously out of date in 6 months time, or might not be your thing in the first place! Also, some of the stuff we've acquired from our various suppliers may no longer be available by the time you read this. We hope that, despite this, our approach of showing you step-by-step how to fit the various parts will mean that, even if the parts change slightly, the procedures we show for fitting will still be valid.

Our main project car was a 1.6 XS, 1997 R reg.

"Wheels & tyres"
takes a detailed
look at all the
options.

"Body styling"
shows you how
to fit anything
from mirrors to
full body kits.

"Interiors"
includes seats,
painting trim,
gear knobs and
loads more.

Haynes Max Power

PMC 36

The Peugeot 306
a lot to live up to

If the Golf GTI invented the hot
hatchback, then surely the 205 GTI
re-invented it, in 1984. Its exuberant
engine and chuckable handling put
the smile back on many driver's
faces, and all wrapped up in a really
good-looking car. Suddenly, Peugeot
had it all going their way.

The success of the 205 led to problems for Peugeot when it eventually reached the end of its life - how to produce a follow-up as good? Remember, platinum albums and blockbuster movies don't always lead to corking sequels. With the 306, opinion's still divided as to whether Peugeot succeeded, but most of the 205's strengths survived intact, and the new model's still a great driver's car (VW, let's not forget, weren't so lucky when they replaced the Mk 2 Golf). For many lads who'd enjoyed the 205, and who couldn't face downsizing to a Saxo or 106, the choice was clear - the 306 in standard form was another good-looking Pug with curves in all the right places, and just crying out for a helping hand in the wannabe streetfighter department. Success as a modded motor was assured, and the sporty turbo-diesel models (with decent levels of bang for less insurance bucks) were just the icing on the cake. Has the hot hatch been re-re-invented?

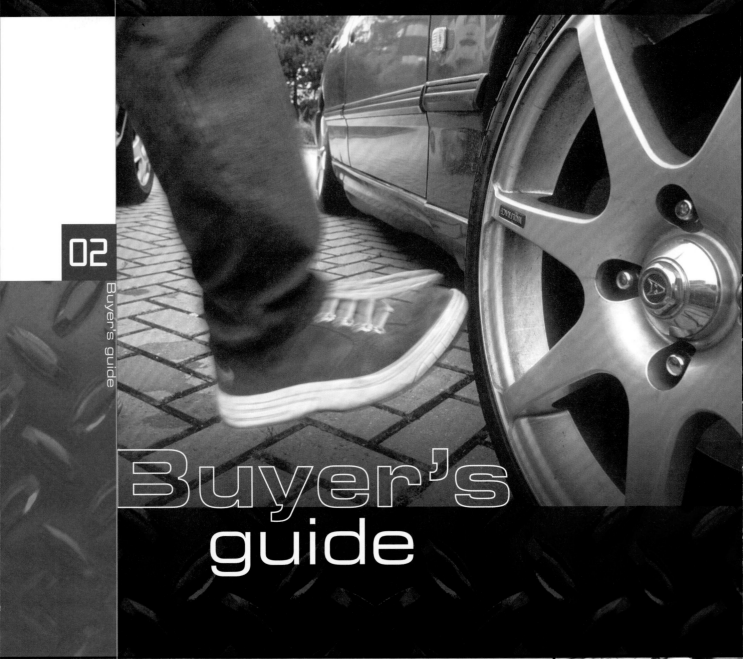

Buyer's guide

What to look for

It's taken a long time, but now 306 secondhand prices are beginning to get more sensible. It's no mystery why the 306 should be so highly-priced (it's a good-looking, quality motor), but now the 307's arrived, this should help to push prices of the original model down further.

In general, the 306 is a solid used buy, with very few problems worth noting. Some have electrical problems on the doors, particularly the window switches. Also, check that's there's good clutch and gearshift operation, as stiff clutches require immediate attention (and expense). Externally, check the rear tyres for uneven wear because with the torsion bar suspension, any kerb slamming or accidents which have knocked one side will also have affected the other. Under the bonnet, a clattering when the engine is cold could indicate poor servicing or high mileage, and you should check for coolant loss as it's a common problem on 306s. An engine that's losing coolant may show white powdery deposits around the cooling system hoses or the radiator, and a car that's being topped-up regularly may now have clear water (as opposed to no water?) in the expansion tank. Also look for leaks on the power steering as this could indicate accident damage on the front end. The dreaded rust wasn't even much of a factor on the 205, so don't expect to see any on a 306 - the only reason you might would be down to badly-repaired crash damage, so walk away.

While the trim on a 306 is reasonably durable, it should still be obvious whether the car's been abused over a long period, or whether the mileage showing is genuine or not - Peugeot trim usually hangs on well enough, but it gets floppy with age (sunroof and window winder handles are a good place to start checking if you're suspicious). Okay, so you may be planning to junk most of the interior at some point, but why should you pay over the odds for a tat car which the owner hasn't given a stuff about? If a scruffy interior doesn't actually put you off, then at least make out that you're not happy about it, and haggle the price down! If you find a really sad example, with dents and faded paint, and a smoky, noisy engine - walk away, unless it's very cheap. There's no point spending most of your budget just to get the car half-tidy before you start the real work on it, surely?

Full service history (fsh)

Is there any service history? If so, this is good, but study the service book carefully:

a *Which garage has done the servcing? Is it a proper dealer, or a backstreet bodger? Do you know the garage, and if so, would you use it?*

b *Do the mileages show a nice even progression, or are there huge gaps? Check the dates too.*

c *Does it look as if the stamps are authentic? Do the oldest ones look old, or could this 'service history' have been created last week, to make the car look good?*

d *When was the last service, and what exactly was carried out? When was the cambelt last changed? Has the owner got receipts for any of this servicing work?*

Don't buy a duffer

Unless you're planning on spending big money on a fairly new 306, it's far better to buy privately, as long as you know what you're doing. Dealers still think they can charge over the odds for Peugeots, but all you'll get for the extra money is a full valet and some degree of comeback if the car's a dog. Buying privately, you get to meet the owner, and this can tell you plenty about how the car's been treated. Everyone's nervous when buying a car, but don't ignore your "gut feelings" when you first see the car, or meet its owner. Also, don't make the common mistake of deciding to buy the car before you've even seen it - too many people seem to make up their minds before setting out, and blindly ignore all the warning signs - remember, there are other cars, and you can walk away!

Take someone who 'knows a bit about cars' along with you - preferably, try and find someone who's either got a 306, or who's had one in the past.

Never buy a car in the dark, or when it's raining. If you do have to view any car in these conditions, agree not to hand over any money until you've seen it in daylight, and when the paintwork's dry (dull, faded paint, or metallic paint that's lost its lacquer, will appear to be shiny in the rain).

One sign of a genuine car is a good batch of old MOTs (assuming it's that old), and as many receipts as possible - even if they're for fairly irrelevant things like tyres (you can see if it's had new tyres, can't you?).

Check that the mileages and dates shown on the receipts and MOTs follow a pattern indicating normal use, with no gaps in the dates, and no sudden drop in the mileage between MOTs (which might suggest the mileage has been 'clocked'). If you are presented with a sheaf of paperwork, it's worth going through it - maybe the car's had a history of problems, or maybe it's just had some nice expensive new parts fitted (like a clutch, starter motor or alternator, for instance).

Check the chassis number (VIN number) and engine number on the registration document and on the car. Any sign of welding near

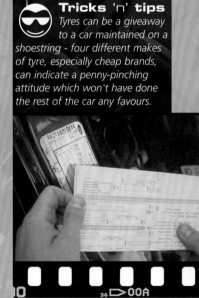

Tricks 'n' tips
Tyres can be a giveaway to a car maintained on a shoestring - four different makes of tyre, especially cheap brands, can indicate a penny-pinching attitude which won't have done the rest of the car any favours.

one of these numbers should be treated with suspicion - to disguise the real number, a thief will run a line of weld over the old number, grind it flat, then stamp in a new number. Other scams include cutting the section of bodywork with the numbers on from another car, then cutting and welding this section into place. The VIN number appears on the VIN plate tucked inside the boot, at the back inner edge; if there is any sign that this plate has been tampered with, walk away - the car could be stolen. The chassis number on this plate should match the one stamped into the right-hand inner wing, under the bonnet - again, if the numbers don't match, or if they're not in a straight line, leave the car well alone - it could be a "ringer" (a stolen car with a fake I.D.). Later models should also have the same VIN etched into the front and rear screens - a windscreen could've been legitimately replaced by now, but a rear window? I think not.

The engine number is stamped onto a flat machined surface on the engine, or else appears on a shiny riveted plate on the engine. This number can be difficult to spot, but keep looking until you find it - if the number's been ground off, or if there's anything suspicious about it, you could be buying trouble.

Check the registration document very carefully - all the details should match the car. If buying privately, make sure that it's definitely the owner's name and address printed on it - if not, be very careful! If buying from a dealer, note the name and address, and try to contact the previous owner to confirm mileage, etc, before handing over more than a deposit. Unless the car's very old, it should not have had too many previous owners - if it's into double figures, it may mean that the car is trouble, so checking its owner history is more important.

306s resist rust pretty well, but don't assume they don't rust at all - check the vulnerable bits like sills, door edges and body seams. Any other body damage should be cheap enough to repair (doors, bonnets and tailgates, etc, are all available from scrapyards by now) so don't panic, just haggle.

Although you may feel a bit stupid doing it, check simple things too, like making sure the windows and sunroof open and shut, and that all the doors and tailgate can be locked. Check all the basic electrical equipment too, as far as possible - lights, front and rear wipers, heated rear window, heater fan; it's amazing how often these things are taken for granted by buyers! If your chosen 306 already has alloys fitted, does it have locking wheel bolts? Where's the key?

Tricks 'n' tips

If your understanding of the mechanical workings of the modern automobile is a bit vague and you want a second opinion, it may also be worth considering having the vehicle inspected. The AA and RAC offer this service, but there may be other people in your area too - check in the Yellow Pages. This is a bit pricier than the vehicle check, but will give you peace of mind and some comeback should things not be as expected. If you've got a friendly garage, maybe they could be persuaded to check the car over for a small fee.

Sealing the deal

Everything as expected and the car's just what you want? It's time to start haggling. Never just agree to hand over the full advertised price for the car, but don't be too ambitious, either (it's best to stay friendly at this point - winding-up the owner is the last thing you need). If the ad says "o.n.o.", expect at least 10% off - if not, why bother putting it on the ad? Try a low offer to test the owner's reaction (they can only say no!) then reluctantly increase the offer until you're both happy. Haggling can also include other considerations besides cash - will the owner chuck in the nice stereo and wheels, leave the tax on, or put a new MOT ("ticket") on it?

Bagged a bargain? Sorted! Offer to leave a deposit (this shows you're serious), but before parting with any more cash, it may be worth considering the following.

Ask for time to get in touch with the previous owner shown on the "logbook" (registration document). If you can speak to them, it's a useful exercise in confirming the car's history and mileage.

A wise thing to do is to run a vehicle check on the car with an organisation such as HPI or the AA. It'll cost you (usually around the 30-quid mark) but could save a lot of hassle in future. They'll need the details of all the identification numbers on the vehicle and documents, as well as the mileage, etc. For your money, they'll run the details of the car through their computer database. This database contains the records of all vehicles reported stolen, which have been total losses (ie. have been totalled after a serious accident) or have outstanding finance against them. They can then confirm over the phone the vehicle is straight, and in theory you can proceed with the deal, safe in the knowledge you're not about to purchase a ringer. Not only will you receive a nice certificate through the post with your vehicle details on it, but running the check also gives you financial insurance. The information given is guaranteed (usually to the tune of about ten grand) so if Plod turns up on your doorstep a month later, demanding you return your new vehicle to its rightful owner, you should be able to claim your cash back. No worries.

Model guide

The good thing about owning a 306 is that, even if it's the smallest output base model, it's still a good car to drive. The great ride quality, excellent handling and responsive steering make it a decent driver's car and one of the best among all modern hatches. All are fuel injection, all come with five-speed gearboxes and independent suspension, but sadly all have a restrictive catalytic converter as they were produced from 1993 onwards. Best body shape to opt for is the 3-door hatch as this has stiffest shell and best handling.

Base 1.4 and 1.6 litre models

The range starts off in with a 1.4 litre engine, which uses single-point injection. This means that the fuel is injected at one source - the top of the intake manifold. Multi-point injection, as on some later larger-engined models, means there's an injector on every intake port, which gives more power.

At 1400cc, the smallest engine manages okay with 75bhp output. This might not set the tyres on fire, but it will give reasonable enough performance, and with the engine freed up a bit (new air filter and back box) it'll at least be a willing revver. Its main advantage is, of course, cheaper insurance and thanks to a group 4 rating it should get almost anyone on the road. It'll also do over 40 mpg on a run, so can get you around without emptying your wallet too.

The 1.4, like all manual 306s apart from the GTI-6, has a five-speed gearbox and this is the transmission to go for. Whatever you do, don't accept an auto because they're unresponsive and uninvolving. Like swimming with wellies on.

The 1.6 litre is more punchy with 90bhp and at only one or two groups higher on insurance, it shouldn't cost much more either. It will certainly give a much better response to any mods you make and isn't too bad on fuel, returning 39mpg.

1.8 and 2.0 litre models

The biggest surprise with the 1.8 litre model is that some insurance companies rate it in the same group as the 1.6 litre, yet it puts out an extra 13bhp at 103bhp. If you're unlucky it might be one group higher, and any 1.8 16V, available from '97 on, will definitely be higher by at least one group, possibly two. This shows that it's well worth shopping around to find cover, as it could make a 1.8 as cost-effective as a 1.6.

The 2.0 litre comes in 8-valve form for 123bhp on '93-'97 models, and manages 135bhp as a 16-valve from '97 up, making it very lively but still reasonable on gas at 30mpg. But if getting the most from a tankful is the aim, you want to look for a turbo, turbo-diesel that is.

1.9 DTurbo model

A rattly old oil-burner? No way, right? Err, yes way. In fact you'll only have to witness a turbo-diesel 306 pulling away from you at speed to be convinced. While the non-turbo diesel might a bit tame, the comparably big torque output of the turbo model makes it a good performer and a wise choice. Power is good at 90bhp, but it's the torque that's impressive here. The turbo gives a 145lb ft output to match the GTI-6, and brings it in lower down the rev range to make everyday driving really responsive. Best of all, you'll only pay the same as a 1.6 model for insurance and you get 42mpg.

S-16, Rallye and GTI-6 models

If you're after one of these models, you'll probably know they represent some of the best hot hatches money can buy. But speed ain't cheap and these models are very sought after, so be prepared to pay the most of any 306 (bar a Cabriolet) particularly for the GTI-6 because of that 6-speed 'box.

The S-16 ran with 155bhp, putting it well above the 2.0 litre XSi, but both the GTI-6 and Rallye go better still with 167bhp at their disposal, and being over 50kg lighter the Rallye is even 0.7 seconds faster to 100mph. These cars really are the 306 daddies, and will cost you for the privilege, with group 15 or 16 insurance.

306
model
history

Like many car ranges in recent years, there's also been a fair number of "special edition" 306 models offered. The models listed are a representative selection - to have listed them all would've taken half the book! Don't pay over the odds for a special edition, unless it's genuinely got some extra kit you're interested in having - most are just the base models with stickers and er... interesting seat trim!

April 1993 (K reg)

Peugeot 306 introduced - choice of 1.4i, 1.6i, 1.8i petrol engines introduced, 1.8 XT model has discs all around with ABS optional on all. Top range XT has twin headlamps and 6-speaker stereo.

July 1993

1.9TD (turbo diesel) 3-door model launched.

January 1994 (L reg)

2.0 XSi and S-16 3-door models launched with power steering, rear spoiler, central locking, electric windows and mirrors, sports seats. S-16 has alloys and ABS.

February 1994

XN 1.4, XL 1.4 and XS 1.6 petrol models, plus XNd 1.9 and 1.9 turbo diesel launched. XS and turbo diesel have tinted glass, power steering, colour-coded bumpers, rear spoiler, fog lamps, sports seats, three-spoke wheel and electric windows.

May 1994

2.0 cabriolet launched with, power steering, ABS, electric hood/windows, sport seats, security system and alloys.

August 1994 (M reg)

Petrol models from XL upwards have keypad immobiliser, and models from XR and XLdt upwards have driver's air bag.

October 1995 (N reg)

XSi upgraded with ABS, alloys, leather steering wheel.

December 1995

Special edition 1.9 turbo diesel S 3-door model launched.

June 1996 (P reg)

Special edition 1.6 XS-S 3-door model launched.

July 1996

GTI-6 2.0 litre 16V 3-door launched with ABS, new alloys and six-speed manual gearbox.

April 1997

Range revised with new headlights, grille, bigger bumpers (body coloured), new doors and side-impact protection, new instrument panel. 2.0 litre 16V (135bhp) replaces 8V on XSi. All models except L have sunroof or air con.

September 1997 (R reg)

New 1.9 diesel turbo S 3-door model launched.

February 1998

CD autochanger on XSi models, CD plus Alcantara/leather trim on GTI-6.

August 1998 (S reg)

1.8 litre XS 3-door model launched.

November 1998

Special edition 2.0 litre Rallye 3-door launched, 50 kg (112 lb) lighter than GTI-6.

June 1999 (T reg)

Range revised with new lights, fog lights, indicators, metal-look dash, aluminium gearstick. TD model uses common-rail diesel.

Performance figures

	0-60 (sec)	Top speed (mph)
1.4	12.9	103
1.6	11.1	110
1.8	10.2	114
1.9 TD	11.2	108
2.0 XSi	9.8	119
2.0 GTI-6	7.9	130
2.0 Rallye	7.8	130

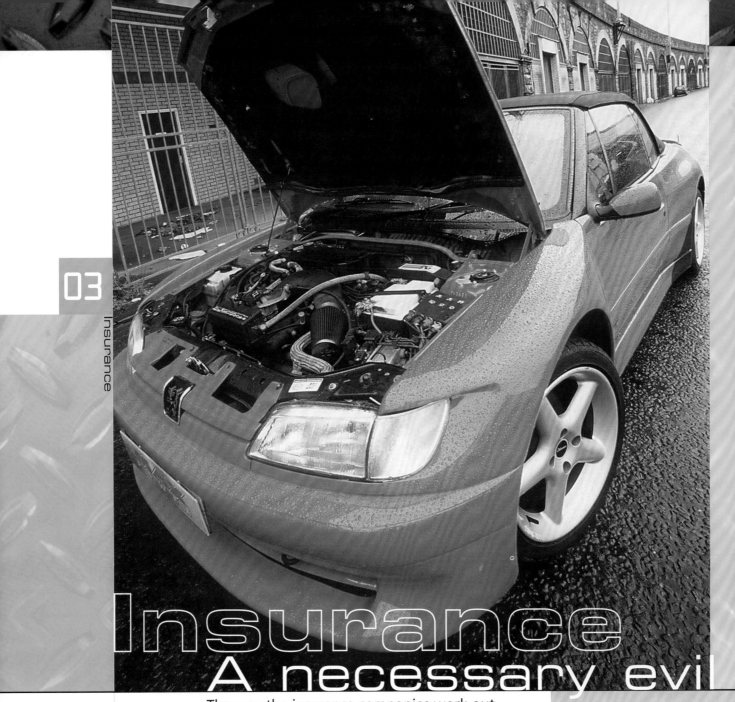

Insurance
A necessary evil

The way the insurance companies work out premiums and assess risks is a mystery to most of us. In general, the smaller the engine you have in your 306, the less you'll pay for insurance, so hopefully, a 1.4 Style will be lots less to insure than a 2.0 GTI-6. However, different companies can give wildly different quotes so it's vital to shop around. Always ring as many brokers and get as many quotes as you possibly can. A few extra minutes spent on the phone once a year may result in an extra few hundred quid in your back pocket.

With modified cars, insurance becomes even more of a problem. By modifying a car, you're making it more of a target for thieves (yes, ok, I know you know this). The point is, the insurance companies know this too, and they don't want to be paying out for the car, plus all the money you've spent on it, should it go missing. There is a temptation 'not to tell the insurance' about the mods you've made. Let's deal with this right now. Our experience has been that, while it can be painful, honesty is best. If they find out (and if you have a claim, they may well come and inspect the car) they won't pay out a penny. And if you do make a claim, very few insurers pay out for the modifications, so you get paid out, but based on a standard car. There are many specialist insurers who are more friendly towards fully-loaded cars, but even they won't actually cover the cost of replacement goodies.

Valuing your car

When your insurance pays out in the event of a total loss or write-off, they base their offer on the current market value of an identical standard model to yours. The only way you'll get more than the average amount is to prove your 306 is in above-average nick (with photos) or that the mileage was especially low for the year.

With this in mind, don't bother over-valuing your Pug in the hope you'll get more in the event of a claim - you won't! The only way to do this is to seek out an "agreed-value" deal, which you can usually only get on classic-car policies (with these, the car's value is agreed in advance between you, not worked out later by the company with you having no say in it). By over-valuing your car, you could be increasing your premium without gaining any benefit.

Equally though, don't under-value, in the hope you'll get a reduction in premium. You won't, and if there's a total loss claim, you won't get any more than your under-valued amount, no matter how loudly you complain.

Work on what you paid for the car, backed up with the sort of prices you see for similar cars in the ads (or use a secondhand car price guide). Add no more than 10% for the sake of optimism, and that's it.

What type of cover?

For most of us, cost means there's only one option - TPF&T (third party, fire and theft). Fully-comp insurance is an unattainable dream for most people until they reach the "magic" age of 25, but what's the real story?

Third Party only

The most basic cover you can get. Basically covers you for damage to other people's cars or property, and for personal injury claims. Virtually no cover for your own stuff, beyond what you get if you take the optional "legal protection" cover.

Third Party, Fire and Theft

As above, with cover for fire and theft, of course! Better, but not much better. This is really only cover in the event of a "total loss", if your car goes missing or goes up in smoke. Still no cover for your car if you stack it into a tree, or if someone breaks in and pinches your stereo.

Fully-comprehensive

In theory, covers you for any loss or damage. Will cover the cost of repairing or replacing your car regardless of whether it was your fault or not. With a fully-comp policy, you can "protect" your no-claims bonus for a small fee so you don't automatically lose those hard-earned years' worth of discount if you prang it All this extra cover costs more, but is often a better bet in the long run.

Your car, or your Dad's?

Don't pretend your sorted 306 belongs to your Dad, and get him to insure it, with you as a named driver. Insurance companies are not stupid. They know that your Dad isn't likely to be running around in a modified car, and they treat any "named driver" application with great suspicion in these cases. This dubious practice also does you no favours in future years. All the time you're living the lie, you're not building up any no-claims bonus of your own.

Not telling the insurance the whole truth gets a little tricky when you have to make a claim. You may think your insurance company is there for your benefit, but they're a business like any other, and their main aim in life is to make money. If the insurance assessor comes around to check your bent/burnt/stolen-and-recovered "standard" Peugeot and finds he's looking at a vehicle fitted with alloys/bodykit/modified interior, he's not going to turn a blind eye.

Limit your premium

When you phone for a quote your fate is pretty much sealed, but there are a few things you can do to help lower the premium

Golden Rule Number One

If in doubt, declare everything. Insurance companies are legally entitled to dispute any claim if the car is found to be non-standard in any way.

Golden Rule Number Two

Before modifying the car, ring your insurance, and ask them how it will affect things.

Fit an approved alarm or immobiliser

In general, any alarm or immobiliser with a Thatcham rating should be recognised by any insurance company, but it pays to check before fitting. In some cases, the discounts offered are not that great any more - but an alarm is still a nice way to get peace of mind.

Avoid speed cameras and The Law

Yes, okay, easier said than done! One SP30 isn't usually too bad, but much more and you'll pay for it, so go easy.

Make yourself the only driver

Pretty self-explanatory. The more people who drive your car, the greater the risk to the company. If you've built up 2 years' worth of no-claims, but your partner hasn't, putting them on your insurance will bump it up, due to their relative inexperience.

Build up your no-claims bonus

You'll only do this by owning and insuring a car in your own name, and then not making any claims. Simple really. Each claim free year you have will aid lowering how much you pay out.

Hang onto your no-claims bonus

Obviously, the less you claim, the less your insurance will cost. If something happens to your car, don't be in too big a hurry to make a claim before you've thought it all through. How much will it cost to fix? How much is your excess? If you can afford not to claim, then don't do it.

Limit your mileage

Most companies offer a discount if you only cover a small annual mileage. To get any meaningful reduction, the mileage has to be less than 10,000 per year. Don't try and pretend you only do 3000 if it's nearer 20,000. Few companies ever ask what the car's current mileage is - so how are they gonna know if you've gone over your self-imposed limit? But if they do find out you could be in trouble.

Get a garage

If you have access to a garage use it, insurers love a car to be locked away safe and sound at night.

Insurance-friendly mods?

So - what do insurance companies like and dislike, as far as mods go? No two companies will have the same outlook, and your own circumstances will play a big part too.

Engine mods

"Mild" mods, such as induction kits and exhausts don't often change premiums, but just the merest mention of "chipping" can make many companies load the premium, or even completely refuse to offer cover. With complete engine transplants, you may be required to give an engineer's report on the mods before they'll grant cover.

Interior mods

As with bodykits, unless you go absolutely mental it really shouldn't make a difference, but make sure you tell your insurers all the same.

Body mods

Even a tiny rear spoiler can be classed as a "bodykit" (yes, it's daft, but that's how it is). Anything which alters the exterior appearance should be declared. As long as the mods aren't too radical, the jump in premium should be fairly small. If anything at all.

Lights

As they're safety-related, you'll probably get asked for lots of details, but as long as you've kept it sensible (and legal, as far as possible) you'll be fine.

Security

Make sure you mention all security stuff - alarms, immobilisers (including mechanical devices), and locking wheel nuts. Don't tell them you've got a Cat 1 if your alarm really came from Argos, and don't tell them you garage the car at night if it's stuck out in the road; if they find out, you're on your own.

Suspension

Average suspension drops of 30-40mm are fine, go much lower and they may charge you more.

Wheels

The specialist insurers won't mind you having a nice set of alloys, but just about every other insurer will load the premium. Make sure you fit locking wheel bolts.

Brakes

Uprating standard sized discs, maybe with grooved or drilled discs, seldom affects the insurance, but some get a bit twitchy when you start fitting bigger discs and replacement calipers.

Security

It's a sad fact, but making your car attractive to the opposite sex also tends to attract attention of a less-welcome kind from brainless thieves.

Avoiding trouble

Now come on - you're modifying your car to look cool and to be seen in. Not a problem - but be careful where you choose to show your car off, and who to. Be especially discreet, the nearer you get to home - turn your system down before you get near home, for instance, or you'll draw unwelcome attention to where that car with the loud stereo's parked at night.

If you're going out, think about where you're parking - somewhere well-lit and reasonably well-populated is the best bet.

Hands up, who doesn't lock their car when they get petrol? Your insurance company has a term for this, and it's "contributory negligence". In English, this means you won't get a penny if your car goes missing when you haven't locked it.

If you're lucky enough to have a garage, use it and fit extra security to the garage door.

Always use all the security you have, whenever you leave the car, even if it's a bit of a chore fitting a steering lock, just do it.

A word about your stereo

From the moment you bolt on those nice alloys, it's taken as read that you've also got stereo gear that's worth nicking - and the thieves know it. All the discreet installation in the world isn't going to deter them from finding out what's inside that nice motor.

If you have a CD player, don't leave discs or empty CD cases lying around inside the car. 6x9s on the rear shelf are also very inviting to thieves, and very easy to steal. When you're fitting your system, give some thought to the clues you could accidentally leave in plain view. Oxygen-free speaker cable is great stuff, but it's also a bit bright against dark carpets, and is all the clue necessary that you're serious about your speakers.

Most modern sets are face-off or MASK, so if they've got security features like this, use them - take your faceplate off when you leave the car, and take it with you rather than leaving it in the door pocket or glovebox (the first places a thief will look).

Things that go beep in the night

Don't skimp on an alarm, it may never even be put to the test, but if it is, you'll be glad you spent wisely …

The simplest first step to car security is to fake it. It's obviously risky if the thief calls your bluff, but if you really can't afford an alarm just an LED is cheap to buy and easy to fit, and can be rigged to a discreet switch inside the car (we show you how, later on).

Don't overlook the value of so-called "manual" immobilisers, such as steering wheel locks. These are a worthwhile deterrent - a thief not specifically after your car (and yours alone) may move on to an easier target. Some of the items offered may be "Sold Secure" or Thatcham Cat 3, accolades well worth checking out, as it means they've withstood a full-on brute force attack for a useful length of time.

The only way to combat the more determined thief is to go for a well-specified and intelligently-installed alarm. Immobilisers alone have their place, but a pro-fitted immobiliser alone won't stop someone pinching your wheels, or breaking in for the stereo gear.

Finally, one other scam which you might fall victim to. If you find that your alarm is suddenly going off a lot at night, when previously it had been well-behaved, don't ignore the problem. It's an old trick for a thief to deliberately set off your alarm several times, each time hiding when you come out to investigate, then to wait until the fifth or sixth time when you don't reset, leaving him a clear run. If your alarm does keep false-alarming without outside assistance, find out the cause quickly, or your neighbours will quickly become "deaf" to it.

Thatcham categories and meanings:

1 **Cat 1.** For alarms and electronic immobilisers.

2 **Cat 2.** For electronic immobilisers only.

3 **Cat 2-1.** Electronic immobilisers which can be upgraded to Cat 1 alarms later.

4 **Cat 3.** Mechanical immobilisers, eg snap-off steering wheels, locking wheel bolts, window film, steering wheel locks/covers.

5 **Q-class.** Tracking devices.

Other alarm features

Two-stage anti-shock - means that the alarm shouldn't go off, just because the neighbour's cat jumps on your car roof, or because Little Johnny punts his football into your car. Alarm will only sound after a major shock, or after repeated shocks are detected.

Anti-tilt - detects any attempt to lift or jack up the car, preventing any attempt to pinch alloys. Very unpopular with thieves, as it makes the alarm very sensitive (much more so than anti-shock). Alarm may sound if car is parked outside in windy conditions (but not if your suspension's rock-hard!).

Anti-hijack - immobiliser with built-in delay. If your motor gets hi-jacked, the neanderthals responsible will only get so far down the road before the engine cuts out.

Rolling code - reduces the chance of your alarm remote control signal from being "grabbed" by special electronic equipment.

Total closure - module which connects to electric windows or sunroof and central locking, which closes all items when alarm is set.

Pager control - yes, really - your alarm can be set to send a message to your pager (why not your mobile?) if your car gets tampered with.

Current-sensing disable - very useful feature on some cars which have a cooling fan which can cut in after the ignition is switched off. Without this feature, your alarm will be triggered every time you leave it parked after a long run - very annoying.

Volumetric-sensing disable - basically allows you to manually disable the interior ultrasonics, leaving the rest of the alarm features active. Useful if you want to leave the sunroof open in hot weather - if a fly gets in the car, the alarm would otherwise be going off constantly.

Talking alarms - no, please, please no. Very annoying, and all that'll happen is you'll attract crowds of kids daring each other to set it off again. Unfortunately, these are becoming more popular, with some offering the facility to record your own message!

The knowledge

What people often fail to realise (at least, until it happens to them) is the level of violence and destruction which thieves will employ to get your stuff - this goes way beyond breaking a window.

It comes as a major shock to most people when they discover the serious kinds of tools (weapons) at many professional thieves' disposal, and how brutally your lovingly-polished car will be attacked. Many people think, for instance, that it's their whole car they're after, whereas it's really only the parts they want, and they don't care how they get them (this means that these parts are still attractive, even when fitted to a basic car which has yet to be fully modded). Obviously, taking the whole car then gives the option of hiding it to strip at leisure, but it won't always be the option chosen, and you could wake up one morning to a well-mangled wreck outside.

Attack 1 The first option to any thief is to smash glass - typically, the toughened-glass side windows, which will shatter, unlike the windscreen. Unfortunately for the thief, this makes a loud noise (not good), but is a quick and easy way in. The reason for taking this approach is that a basic car alarm will only go off if the doors are opened (voltage-drop alarm) - provided the doors aren't opened, the alarm won't go off.

Response 1 A more sophisticated alarm will feature shock sensing (which will be set off by the impact on the glass), and better still, ultrasonic sensing, which will be triggered by the brick coming in through the broken window.

Response 2 This kind of attack can also be stopped by applying security film to the inside of the glass, which holds it all together and prevents easy entry.

Attack 2 An alternative to smashing the glass is to pry open the door using a crowbar - this attack involves literally folding open the door's window frame by prising from the top corner. The glass will still shatter, but as long as the door stays shut, a voltage-drop alarm won't be triggered.

Response This method might not be defeated by a shock-sensing alarm, but an ultrasonic unit would pick it up.

Incidentally, another bonus with ultrasonic alarms is that the sensors are visible from outside - and act as a deterrent.

Attack 3 The next line of attack is to disable the alarm. The commonest way to kill the alarm is either to cut the wiring to the alarm itself, or to disconnect the battery after taking a crowbar to your bonnet catch.

Response 1 If your alarm has extra pin-switches, be sure to fit one to the bonnet, and fit it in the bonnet channel next the battery, so that it'll set off the alarm if the bonnet is prised up. Also make sure that the wire to the pin-switch cannot be cut easily though a partly-open bonnet.

Response 2 Make sure that the alarm module is well-hidden, and cannot be got at from underneath the car.

Response 3 Make the alarm power supply connection somewhere less obvious than directly at the battery terminal - any thief who knows his stuff will immediately cut any "spare" red wires at the battery. Try taking power from the fusebox, or if you must source it under the bonnet, trace the large red battery lead to the starter motor connections, and tap into the power there.

Response 4 Always disguise the new alarm wiring, by using black insulating tape to wrap it to the existing wiring loom. Tidying up in this way also helps to ensure the wires can't get trapped, cut, melted, or accidentally ripped out - any of which could leave you with an alarm siren which won't switch off, or an immobiliser you can't disable.

Response 5 An alarm which has a "battery back-up" facility is best. Even if he's successfully crow-barred your bonnet and snipped the battery connections, the alarm will still go off, powered by a separate battery of its own. A Cat 1 alarm has to have battery back-up.

Fitting a basic LED

All you need for this is a permanent live feed, an earth, a switch if you want to be able to turn it on/off, and the flashing LED itself (very cheap, from any car accessory shop).

An LED draws very little current, so tap into almost any live feed you fancy. If you've wired in your ICE, take a live feed from the permanent (radio memory supply) wire at the back of your head unit, or go into the fusebox (as featured in the alarm fitting procedure). An earth can easily be tapped again from your head unit, or you can make one almost anywhere on the metal body of the car - drill a small hole, fit a self-tapping screw, then wrap the bared end of wire around and tighten it.

The best place to mount an LED is into one of the blank switches the makers love fitting. The blank switch is pried out, and a hole can then be drilled to take the LED (which comes in a separate little holder). Feed the LED wiring down behind the dashboard to where you've tapped your live and earth, taking care not to trap it anywhere, nor to accidentally wrap it around any moving parts.

Connect your live to the LED red wire, then rig your earth to one side of the switch, and connect the LED black wire to the other switch terminal. You should now have a switchable LED! Tidy up the wiring, and mount the switch somewhere discreet, but where you can still get at it. Switch on when you leave the car, and it looks as if you've got some sort of alarm - better than nothing!

Wiring
basics

If you were thinking of taking an alarm live supply direct from the battery - don't. It's better to trace the red lead down to the starter motor, and tap in there.

If a thief manages to get past your bonnet switch, his first thought will be to cut every additional live feed at the battery - of course, if he cuts all the battery leads, you're stuffed (without a battery back-up alarm), but at least you tried…

With your wires identified, how to tap into them?

The best options are:

Soldering - avoids cutting through your chosen wire - strip away a short section of insulation, wrap your new wire around the bared section, then apply solder to secure it. If you're a bit new to soldering, practice on a few offcuts of wire first.

Bullet connectors - cut and strip the end of your chosen wire, wrap your new one to it, push both into one half of the bullet. Connect the other end of your victim wire to the other bullet, and connect together. Always use the "female" half on any live feed - it'll be safer if you disconnect it than a male bullet, which could touch bare metal and send your motor up in smoke.

Block connectors - so easy to use. Just remember that the wires can come adrift if the screws aren't really tight, and don't get too ambitious about how many wires you can stuff in one hole (block connectors, like bullets, are available in several sizes).

Steer clear of connectors like the one below – they're convenient but can give rise to problems.

With any of these options, always insulate around your connection - especially when soldering, or you'll be leaving bare metal exposed. Remember that you'll probably be shoving all the wires up into the dark recesses of the under-dash area - by the time the wires are nice and kinked/squashed together, that tiny bit of protruding wire might just touch that bit of metal bodywork, and cause a fire…

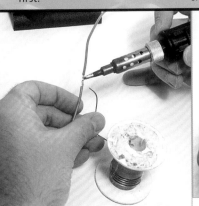

Alarm fitting

Anyone who says they don't need an alarm on their motor is kidding themselves. The speed at which a car can be nicked nowadays defies belief. You only need to be popping into the bank or grabbing a mag from the newsagents to give a thief a chance. So, you need your car protected and you need a system which is advanced enough to give a tealeaf a hard time. Peugeot do their own alarm, called 'Defender'. It's a plug-in upgrade system to the standard immobiliser, and will give your security a Cat 1 rating, to boot.

The Defender has a self-powered siren so it can't be affected by disconnecting the battery (though it takes the batteries in the siren several hours of being connected to charge up), ultrasonic sensors to detect any movement inside the car, which can be switched off via a small button if you leave a pet (or your partner) in the car, and it comes with a bonnet switch to activate the alarm in case the front's prised open with a crowbar.

Fitting the unit is fairly simple, though it can require a couple of 'phone calls to Peugeot technicians, or at least a visit to a dealers, to check out their own VIZ 316 workshop manual which provides a bit more insight into each Peugeot model's wiring. It goes without saying that you need your Haynes manual for its wiring diagrams.

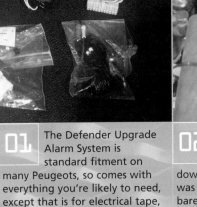

01 The Defender Upgrade Alarm System is standard fitment on many Peugeots, so comes with everything you're likely to need, except that is for electrical tape, wire and terminal crimping tool, a button/switch for the rear hatch, digital multimeter plus some instructions. Not too bad, then...

02 Fit the siren somewhere where it is difficult to get to. We chose low down on the firewall, which was so awkward we could barely get a drill behind the engine to make the two mounting holes.

03 Plug the siren harness in and push the connector's clip into place.

Attention!
When trying to make holes, avoid the very centre of the bulkhead, low down, as this is where the heater matrix is located - put a screwdriver through that, and you won't be a very happy bunny.

The siren harness needs to go through the bulkhead, so drill a 10mm hole for this in the bulkhead and fit a grommet over the harness to prevent any chafing. **04**

The supplied 5-way white connector needs to go on the end of the harness, hence you need your crimping tool at this stage. **05**

Crimp on all the connectors to each of the wires except the blue/black, which can be taped up. **06**

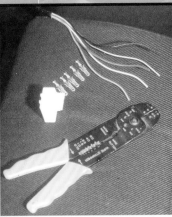

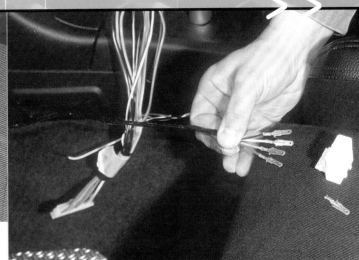

>>

The wires can now be pushed into the connector housing, The orange doesn't get connected on the 306 models so **07** that too should be taped up.

Find a place for this mess. Actually, the wiring harness has many wires which aren't used as the Defender system is made for every type of Peugeot. The alarm unit should be fitted behind the dashboard **08** so it's difficult to get to.

Route the black earth wire from the alarm unit harness through to a suitable earthing point. One can be found on **09** the inner chassis leg, just under the battery.

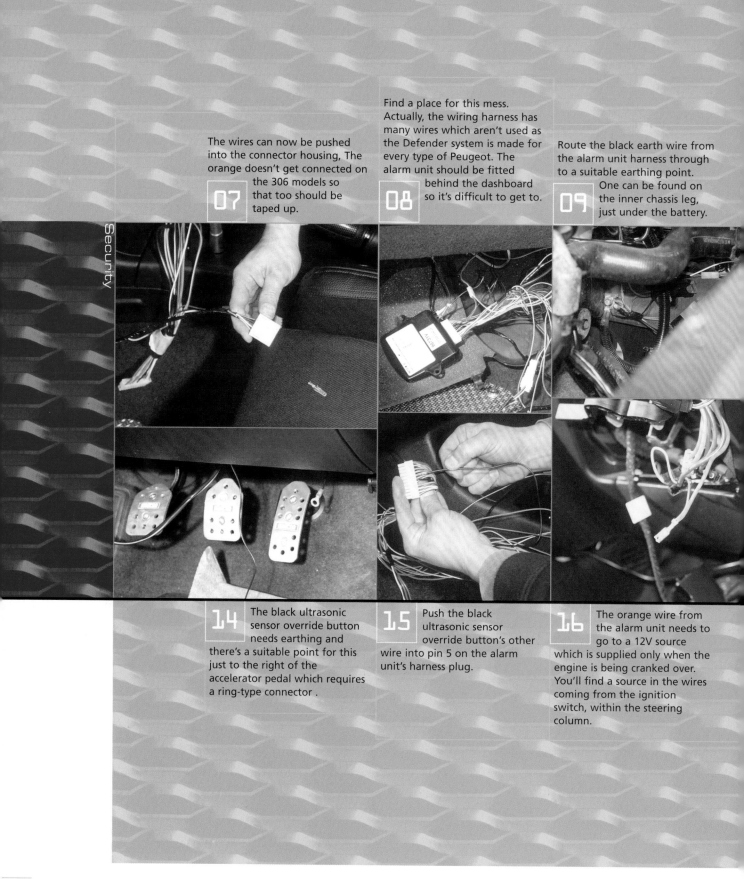

14 The black ultrasonic sensor override button needs earthing and there's a suitable point for this just to the right of the accelerator pedal which requires a ring-type connector .

15 Push the black ultrasonic sensor override button's other wire into pin 5 on the alarm unit's harness plug.

16 The orange wire from the alarm unit needs to go to a 12V source which is supplied only when the engine is being cranked over. You'll find a source in the wires coming from the ignition switch, within the steering column.

10 Route the red wire from the alarm unit to suitable constant 12V source, which can be found inside the fuse box next to the battery.

11 The kit comes with an LED and small button to allow the ultrasonic sensors to be switched off in case you leave a dog or other pet inside the car. These need to be mounted on the dash somewhere conspicuous.

12 We found the best place and easiest to access was the panel to the right of the steering column as it pops out and has space behind it.

13 Connect the LED wires via the brown plug and route the cable behind the dash to your alarm control unit position.

17 The yellow wires from the alarm unit need to go to the right and left indicator, to flash them when the alarm is activated. The best source is the hazard light switch on the dash.

18 Using the blue connectors supplied, attach the yellow wires to the beige and white wires coming from the switch. These are the feeds for the front/rear/side indicators either side, hence it doesn't matter which way around these attach.

19 The ultrasonic sensors have come with the mounting brackets and wire. Each also has a plug which fits into the back of the alarm unit.

>>

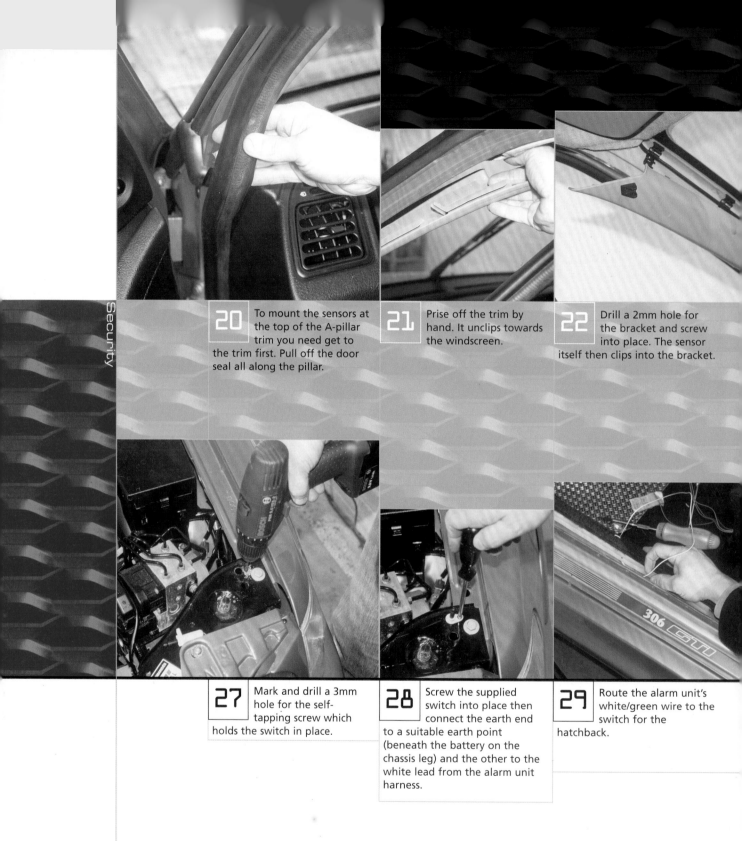

20 To mount the sensors at the top of the A-pillar trim you need get to the trim first. Pull off the door seal all along the pillar.

21 Prise off the trim by hand. It unclips towards the windscreen.

22 Drill a 2mm hole for the bracket and screw into place. The sensor itself then clips into the bracket.

27 Mark and drill a 3mm hole for the self-tapping screw which holds the switch in place.

28 Screw the supplied switch into place then connect the earth end to a suitable earth point (beneath the battery on the chassis leg) and the other to the white lead from the alarm unit harness.

29 Route the alarm unit's white/green wire to the switch for the hatchback.

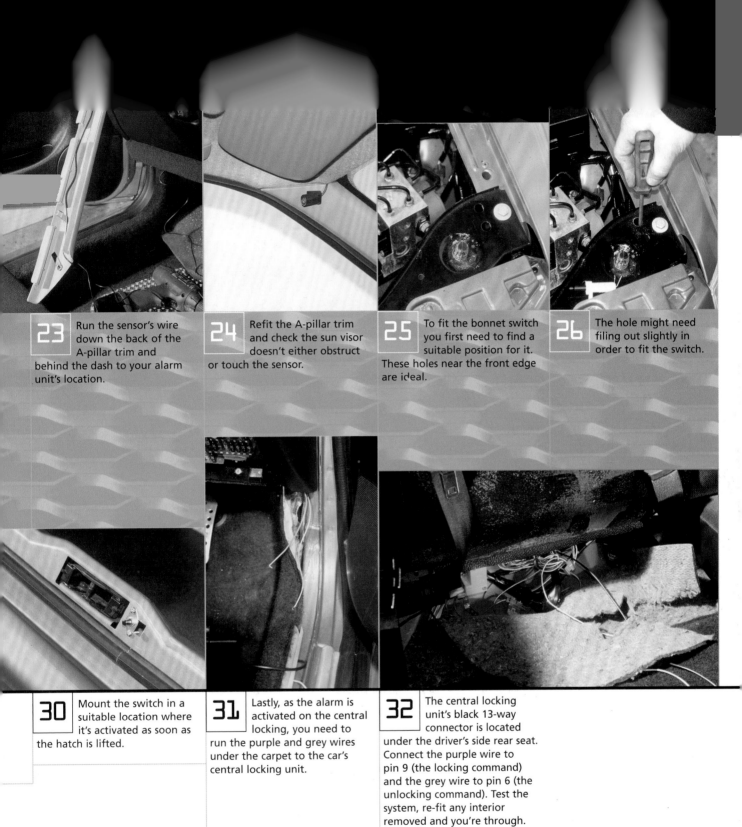

23 Run the sensor's wire down the back of the A-pillar trim and behind the dash to your alarm unit's location.

24 Refit the A-pillar trim and check the sun visor doesn't either obstruct or touch the sensor.

25 To fit the bonnet switch you first need to find a suitable position for it. These holes near the front edge are ideal.

26 The hole might need filing out slightly in order to fit the switch.

30 Mount the switch in a suitable location where it's activated as soon as the hatch is lifted.

31 Lastly, as the alarm is activated on the central locking, you need to run the purple and grey wires under the carpet to the car's central locking unit.

32 The central locking unit's black 13-way connector is located under the driver's side rear seat. Connect the purple wire to pin 9 (the locking command) and the grey wire to pin 6 (the unlocking command). Test the system, re-fit any interior removed and you're through.

Body styling

If you're planning a major body job, you've probably already got some good ideas about how you want your 306 to look. While it can be good to have a target car to aim for, if you're just starting out on the road towards a fully-loaded car, you probably don't want (or can't quite afford) to go 'all the way' all at once.

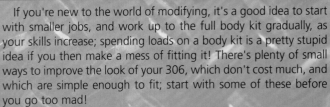

If you're new to the world of modifying, it's a good idea to start with smaller jobs, and work up to the full body kit gradually, as your skills increase; spending loads on a body kit is a pretty stupid idea if you then make a mess of fitting it! There's plenty of small ways to improve the look of your 306, which don't cost much, and which are simple enough to fit; start with some of these before you go too mad!

One golden rule with any body mods is to plan what you're going to do, and don't rush it. It's better that the car looks a bit stupid for a week (because you couldn't get something finished) than to rush a job and have the car look stupid forever. Do half the job properly rather all of it badly. Try and think the jobs through - don't just say to yourself: "Right! Now I'm going to fit those new mirrors!". Read through the instructions (if any), then see what we say, and plan each stage.

Have you got all the tools, screws or whatever before you start, or will you have to break off halfway through? If you get stuck, is there someone you can get to help, or have they gone off for the weekend? Above all, if something goes wrong - don't panic - a calm approach will prove to be a huge bonus (that job doesn't have to be done today, does it?).

Fitting a
sunstrip

Body styling

The modern sunstrip - where did it come from? Could it be a descendant of the eye-wateringly naff old shadebands which were popular in the 70s - you know, the ones which had "DAVE AND SHARON" on? If so, things have only got better...

There are two options to make your car look (and maybe even feel) cooler:

a The sunvisor, a screen tint band inside the screen, which is usually a graduated-tint strip. As this fits inside, there's a problem straight away - the interior mirror. The 306 mirror is bonded to the screen, and it seriously gets in the way when trying to fit a wet and sticky (nice!) strip of plastic around it. Go for a sunstrip instead.

b The sunstrip, which is opaque vinyl, colour-matched to the car, fits to the outside of the screen. Much more Sir.

A really wide sunstrip imitates the "roof chop" look seen on American hot rods, and colour-coded, they can look very effective from the front - plus, of course, you can use the space to advertise your preferred brand of ICE (no, no, NO. Not a good idea!). As it's fitted to the outside of the screen, the sunstrip has a good chance of seriously interfering with your wipers (or wiper, if you've been converted). If this happens to the point where the wipers can't clean the screen, Mr MOT might have a point if he fails your car... The wiper blades may need replacing more often, and the sunstrip itself might start peeling off - still sound like fun?

This is only stuck to the outside, so only the outside of the screen needs cleaning - excellent! Do a good job of cleaning, though - any dirt stuck under the strip will ruin the effect. **01**

Lay the strip onto the screen, and have a mate help you to get it level, and roughly in the required position. **02**

Now measure how much screen you've got left. This strip's gonna be a bit of a badboy, by the look of it. We fought the law, and... **03**

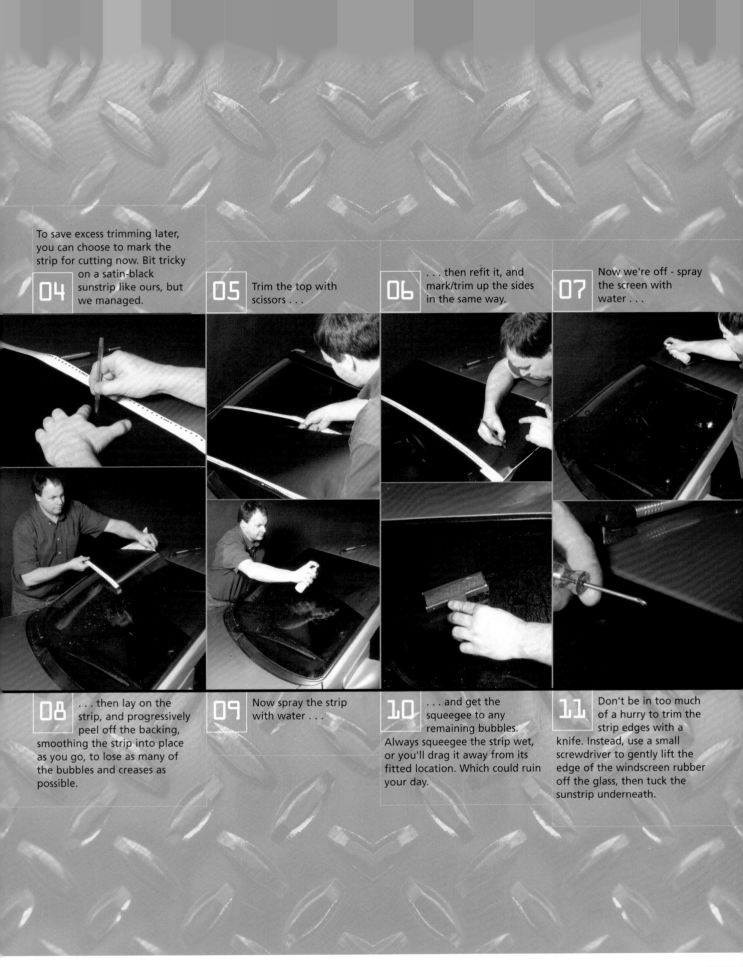

04 To save excess trimming later, you can choose to mark the strip for cutting now. Bit tricky on a satin-black sunstrip like ours, but we managed.

05 Trim the top with scissors . . .

06 . . . then refit it, and mark/trim up the sides in the same way.

07 Now we're off - spray the screen with water . . .

08 . . . then lay on the strip, and progressively peel off the backing, smoothing the strip into place as you go, to lose as many of the bubbles and creases as possible.

09 Now spray the strip with water . . .

10 . . . and get the squeegee to any remaining bubbles. Always squeegee the strip wet, or you'll drag it away from its fitted location. Which could ruin your day.

11 Don't be in too much of a hurry to trim the strip edges with a knife. Instead, use a small screwdriver to gently lift the edge of the windscreen rubber off the glass, then tuck the sunstrip underneath.

Door sills

A simple dress-up item which will also protect your car's paintwork? Look no further than the RGM Styling Sill Protectors. These are simple to fit, good to look at, are available in a number of finishes and have your choice of car model (ie GTi, XSi) engraved on them. Fit them during the ad break on 'Who Wants To Be A Millionaire?'.

01 The RGM Styling door sill protectors are a simple add-on which can be fitted in no time.

02 Pull up the seal all the way along the door sill.

03 Clean the area thoroughly to remove all traces of dirt and grease.

04 Peel the protective layer off the sticky pad on the reverse of the sill protectors.

05 Press the sill well into place, making sure the ends sits on the seams on the 306 sill. Stand back and admire your five-minute modification.

Badge removal

While many cars have their badges positioned in specific holes made in the bodywork at the factory, most Peugeot badges are simply stuck on, thus making them easy to remove. Removing badges smoothes out a car's lines by making them less cluttered, plus it removes the model's identity, so doesn't let on to what you've got to play with.

01 You know what car you've got, so why do you need badges? Exactly. Time to get 'em off.

02 A hairdryer or heatgun makes short work of heating up the glue by which the badges are attached, but it won't affect the paintwork.

03 The hairdryer makes the badge too hot to hold, so use something like a plastic filler spatula to get beneath it without damaging the paint, then gradually peel it off. A quick polish up and car's rear end looks smooth and fat.

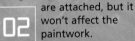
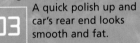

Painting
by numbers

This is not where we tell you how to respray your entire 306 in a weekend, using only spray cans, okay? Mission Impossible, we ain't. This bit's about spraying your various plasticky bits before final fitting - door mirrors, light brows, spoilers, splitters - hell, even bumpers if you like. Always fit your unpainted bits first, to be sure it all fits properly (shape and tidy up all parts as necessary), and that all holes have been drilled. Then, and only when you're totally happy with the fit - take them off, and get the spray cans out.

If you like a wildlife in your paint, you can't beat the great outdoors. If it's windy, you'll get overspray everywhere. Even indoors, if it's damp, you'll never get a shine - a heater is essential (but not a fan heater - stirring up the dust is the last thing you want).

01 Especially with "shiny" plastic, you must rough-up the surface before spray will "bite" to it, or - it'll flippin' flake off. Just take off the shine, no more. You can use fine wet-and-dry for this (used dry), but we prefer Scotch-Brite. This stuff, which looks like a scouring pad, is available from motor factors and bodyshops, in several grades. Remove any unwanted "seams" in the plastic, and tidy up any areas you're not happy with, fit-wise, while you're at it.

02 Mask off any areas you don't want painted - don't be shy with the masking tape, and make sure the edges are well stuck. That said, to avoid a sharp edge of paint (which can look wrong in some cases), the pros stick the tape on lightly, then fold the tape back on itself, lengthways, to present a folded edge of mask to the paint. This creates a softer, though still straight, edge in the paint.

03 Once the surface has been nicely "roughened", clean up the surface using a suitable degreaser ("suitable" means a type which won't dissolve plastic!). Generally, it's ok to use methylated spirit, 'panel wipe' or cellulose thinners (just don't inhale), but test it on a not-so-visible bit first, so you don't have a disaster.

04 Before you start spraying (if it's something smaller than a bumper) it's a good idea to try a work a screw into one of the mounting holes, to use as a "handle", or to hang the piece up from, so you can turn the item to spray all sides. Otherwise, you might need to hold with one (gloved) hand, and spray with the other - messy. Give the paint can a good shake.

05 If you're a bit new at spraying, practice your technique first (steady!). Working left-right, then right-left, press the nozzle so you start spraying just before you pass the item, and follow through just past it the other side. Keep the nozzle a constant distance - not in a curved arc. Don't blast the paint on too thick, or you'll have a nasty case of the runs - hold the can about 6 inches away - you're not trying to paint the whole thing in one sweep.

06 Once you've got a patchy "mist coat" on - stop, and let it dry (primer dries pretty quickly). Build up thin coats until you've got coverage, then let it dry. Using 1000- or 1200-grade wet-and-dry paper (used wet), lightly sand the whole primered surface. Try not to go through the primer to the plastic, but this doesn't matter too much in small areas.

07 Rinse off thoroughly, then dry the surfaces. Make sure the surfaces are clean before continuing with the top coats. As with the primer, work up from an initial thin mist coat, allowing time for each pass to dry. You'll soon learn how to build a nice shine without runs - any "dry" (dull) patches are usually due to overspray landing on still-wet shiny paint. Don't worry if you can't eliminate all of these - a light cutting polish will sort it out, or you can use lacquer.

Side strips

Another nasty item of 'door furniture', the side rubbing strips need attention if you're serious about raising your game. They come off easily on the 306, but leave behind a row of holes and a depression in the panel - could be a bodyshop job to make neat work of taking them off entirely. But don't despair - the strips can be made a lot less offensive by colour-coding.

The 306 has side strips which may be two different depths - the wider one is used only on the posher models, and is available cheaply from Peugeot dealers. Many bodykits assume that the wider strip will be used, and look odd if you keep the thinner strip instead - which is exactly where we were, after our Ecosse kit went on. Something had to be done.

01 The nasty old thin black strip just pops off. Don't worry if some of the clips break, or get left behind - a new strip from Peugeot contains a set of new clips.

02 Here we see the old and the new. The new one has obviously been colour-coded, in a here's-one-we-did-earlier kind of way. Which one would you rather see on your 306? Assuming yours is Blaze Yellow, that is...

03 The new strip has a hooked lug at the front end, so hook it in . . .

04 . . . before pressing the rest of the clips home. What a result.

41

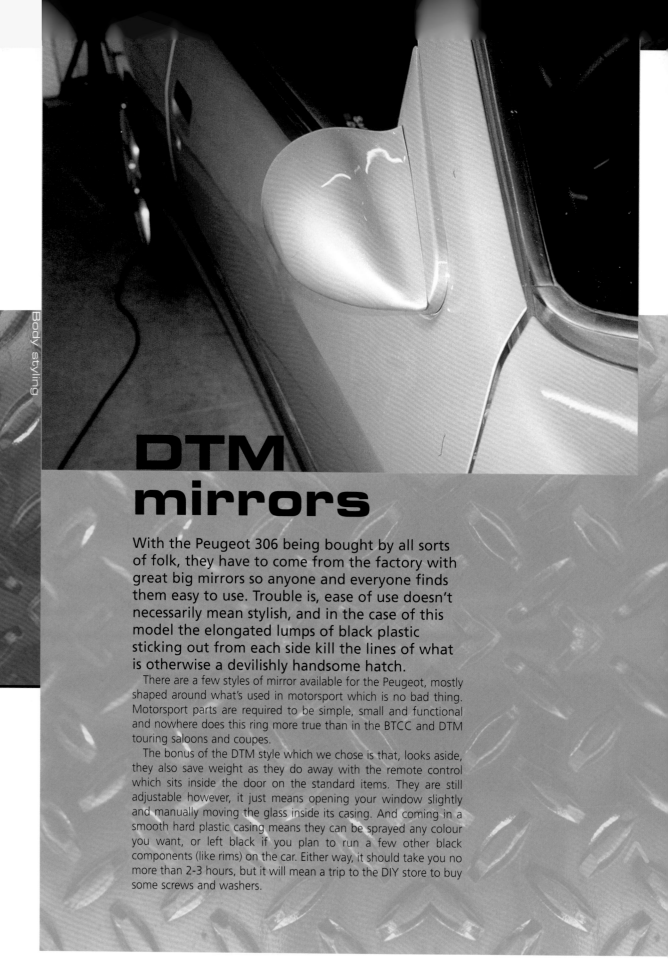

DTM mirrors

With the Peugeot 306 being bought by all sorts of folk, they have to come from the factory with great big mirrors so anyone and everyone finds them easy to use. Trouble is, ease of use doesn't necessarily mean stylish, and in the case of this model the elongated lumps of black plastic sticking out from each side kill the lines of what is otherwise a devilishly handsome hatch.

There are a few styles of mirror available for the Peugeot, mostly shaped around what's used in motorsport which is no bad thing. Motorsport parts are required to be simple, small and functional and nowhere does this ring more true than in the BTCC and DTM touring saloons and coupes.

The bonus of the DTM style which we chose is that, looks aside, they also save weight as they do away with the remote control which sits inside the door on the standard items. They are still adjustable however, it just means opening your window slightly and manually moving the glass inside its casing. And coming in a smooth hard plastic casing means they can be sprayed any colour you want, or left black if you plan to run a few other black components (like rims) on the car. Either way, it should take you no more than 2-3 hours, but it will mean a trip to the DIY store to buy some screws and washers.

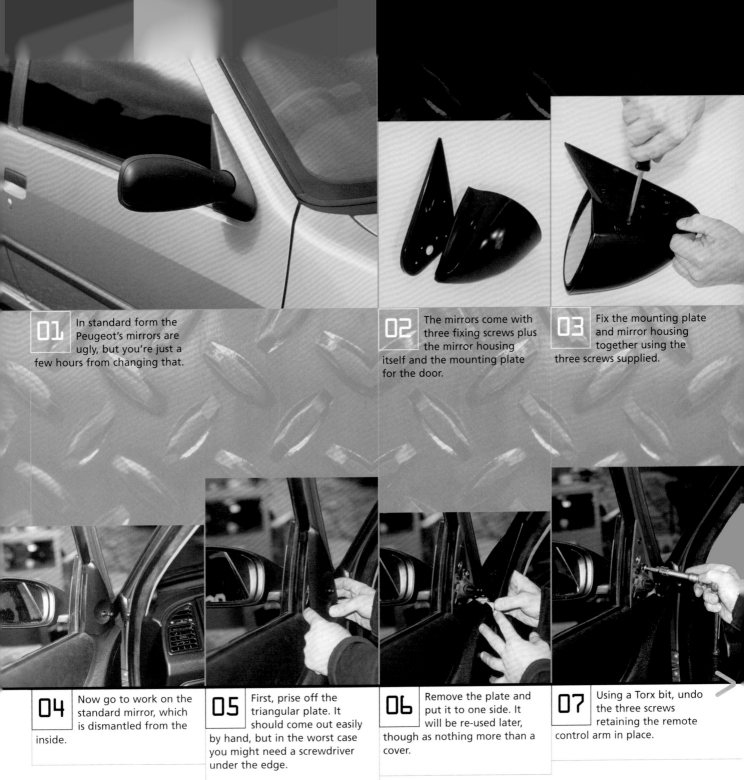

01 In standard form the Peugeot's mirrors are ugly, but you're just a few hours from changing that.

02 The mirrors come with three fixing screws plus the mirror housing itself and the mounting plate for the door.

03 Fix the mounting plate and mirror housing together using the three screws supplied.

04 Now go to work on the standard mirror, which is dismantled from the inside.

05 First, prise off the triangular plate. It should come out easily by hand, but in the worst case you might need a screwdriver under the edge.

06 Remove the plate and put it to one side. It will be re-used later, though as nothing more than a cover.

07 Using a Torx bit, undo the three screws retaining the remote control arm in place.

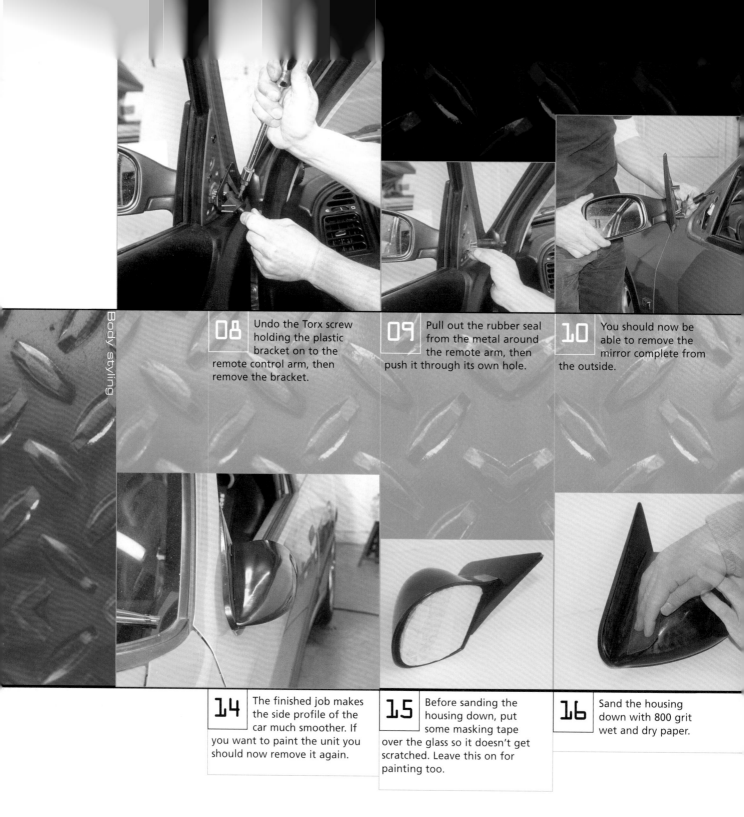

08 Undo the Torx screw holding the plastic bracket on to the remote control arm, then remove the bracket.

09 Pull out the rubber seal from the metal around the remote arm, then push it through its own hole.

10 You should now be able to remove the mirror complete from the outside.

14 The finished job makes the side profile of the car much smoother. If you want to paint the unit you should now remove it again.

15 Before sanding the housing down, put some masking tape over the glass so it doesn't get scratched. Leave this on for painting too.

16 Sand the housing down with 800 grit wet and dry paper.

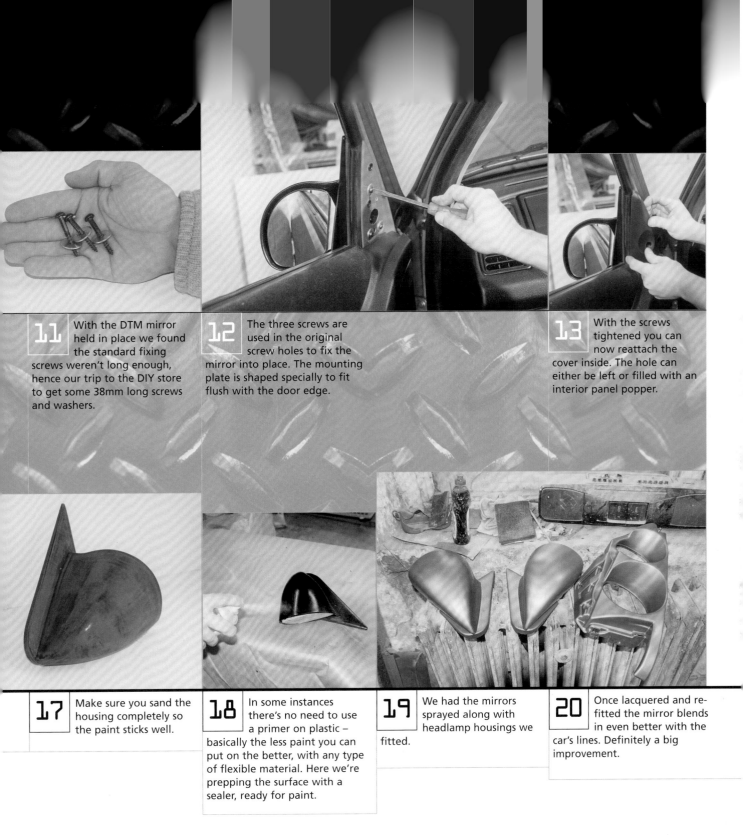

11 With the DTM mirror held in place we found the standard fixing screws weren't long enough, hence our trip to the DIY store to get some 38mm long screws and washers.

12 The three screws are used in the original screw holes to fix the mirror into place. The mounting plate is shaped specially to fit flush with the door edge.

13 With the screws tightened you can now reattach the cover inside. The hole can either be left or filled with an interior panel popper.

17 Make sure you sand the housing completely so the paint sticks well.

18 In some instances there's no need to use a primer on plastic – basically the less paint you can put on the better, with any type of flexible material. Here we're prepping the surface with a sealer, ready for paint.

19 We had the mirrors sprayed along with headlamp housings we fitted.

20 Once lacquered and re-fitted the mirror blends in even better with the car's lines. Definitely a big improvement.

Mesh grille

Mesh is used on all the best sports cars and provides not only a look of performance but also can stop leaves or stones entering the grille area and either blocking an air intake or damaging the radiator. Fitting it is easiest with the front bumper removed but it is possible to fit without doing so.

03 Cut the mesh roughly to size using snips.

04 Cut the corners so the mesh can be folded around the hole in four lengths, one at each side.

05 Push each edge down around the back of the hole.

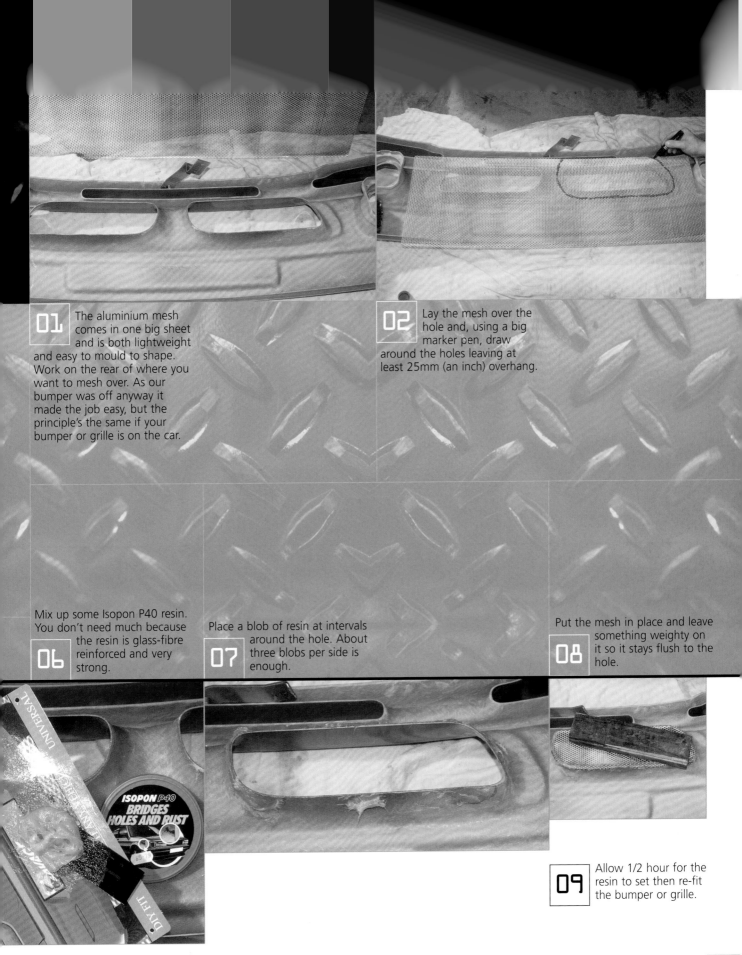

01 The aluminium mesh comes in one big sheet and is both lightweight and easy to mould to shape. Work on the rear of where you want to mesh over. As our bumper was off anyway it made the job easy, but the principle's the same if your bumper or grille is on the car.

02 Lay the mesh over the hole and, using a big marker pen, draw around the holes leaving at least 25mm (an inch) overhang.

Mix up some Isopon P40 resin. You don't need much because the resin is glass-fibre reinforced and very **06** strong.

Place a blob of resin at intervals around the hole. About **07** three blobs per side is enough.

Put the mesh in place and leave something weighty on **08** it so it stays flush to the hole.

09 Allow 1/2 hour for the resin to set then re-fit the bumper or grille.

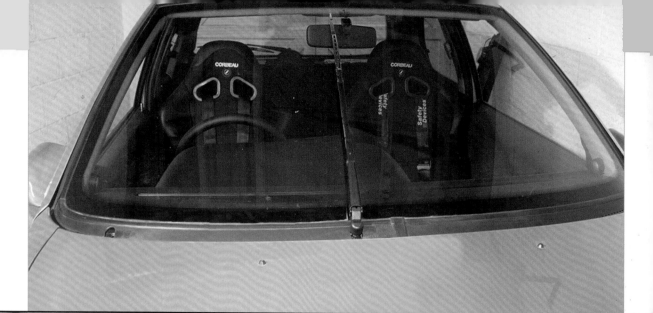

Single wiper conversion

Single wiper conversions are another one of those aftermarket accessories which have made a successful transition from circuit to road cars. Having a single wiper doesn't clean your windscreen better, it doesn't clean any more of it (in fact it sweeps less area) and if you have it parked in the wrong place on your windscreen it's an MoT failure. But damn, it looks good!

Once fitted, to pass an MoT and, strictly speaking, be legal, you need to have the windscreen parked towards the passenger side, lower half of the screen, but we've shown as per the way touring cars run theirs on the circuit, 'cause it's worth the pose value.

 01 The single wiper conversion comes with new motor linkage, wiper arm and huge blade.

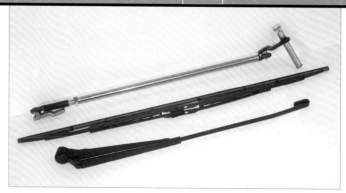

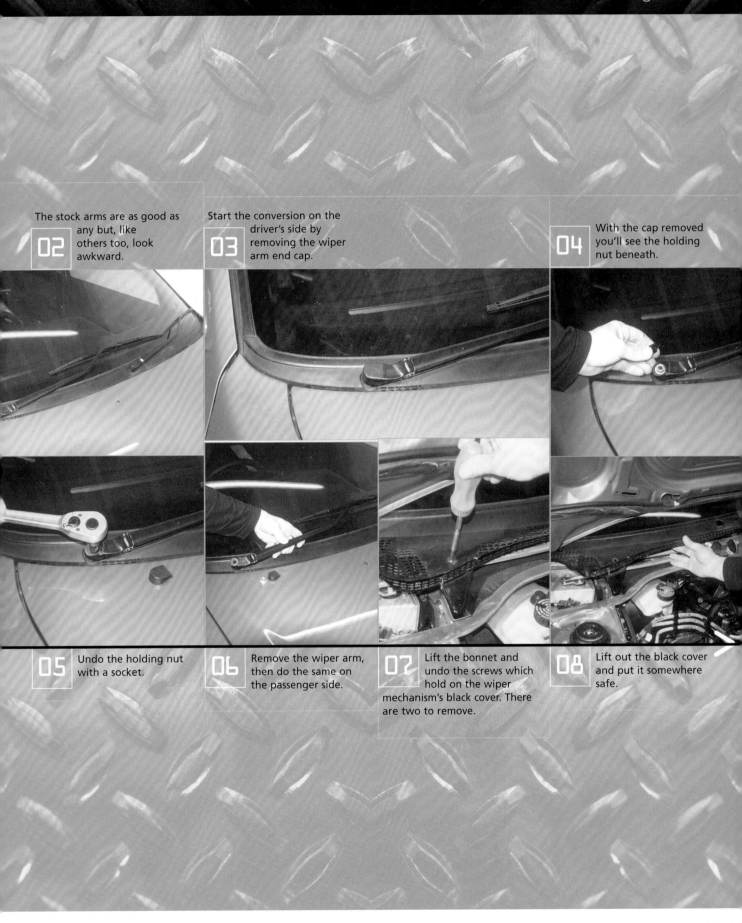

02 The stock arms are as good as any but, like others too, look awkward.

03 Start the conversion on the driver's side by removing the wiper arm end cap.

04 With the cap removed you'll see the holding nut beneath.

05 Undo the holding nut with a socket.

06 Remove the wiper arm, then do the same on the passenger side.

07 Lift the bonnet and undo the screws which hold on the wiper mechanism's black cover. There are two to remove.

08 Lift out the black cover and put it somewhere safe.

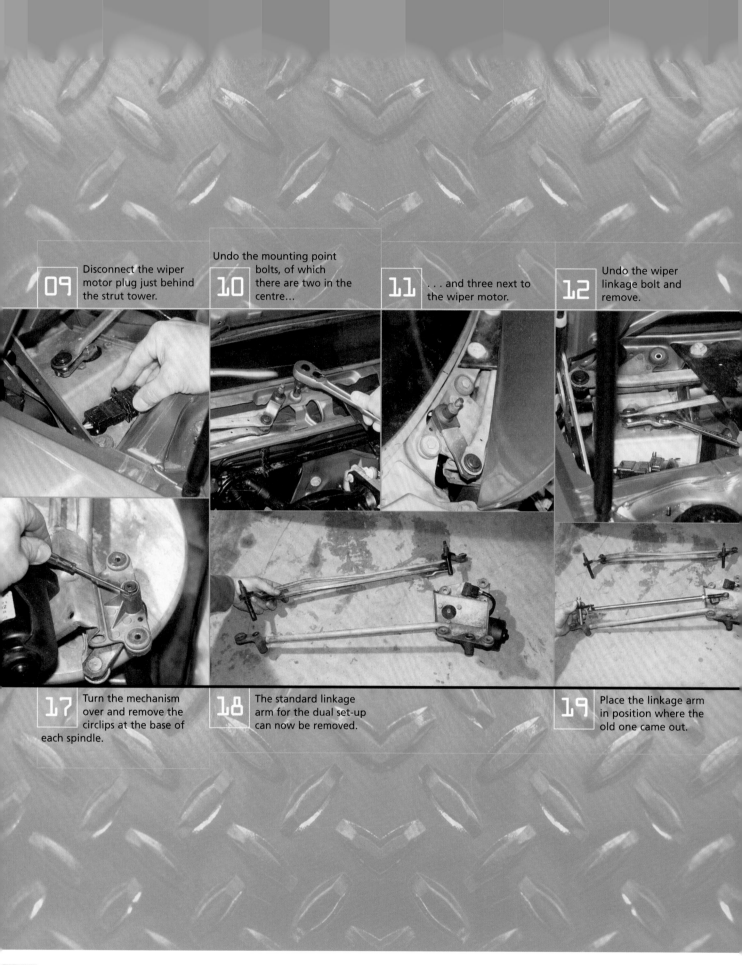

09 Disconnect the wiper motor plug just behind the strut tower.

10 Undo the mounting point bolts, of which there are two in the centre...

11 . . . and three next to the wiper motor.

12 Undo the wiper linkage bolt and remove.

17 Turn the mechanism over and remove the circlips at the base of each spindle.

18 The standard linkage arm for the dual set-up can now be removed.

19 Place the linkage arm in position where the old one came out.

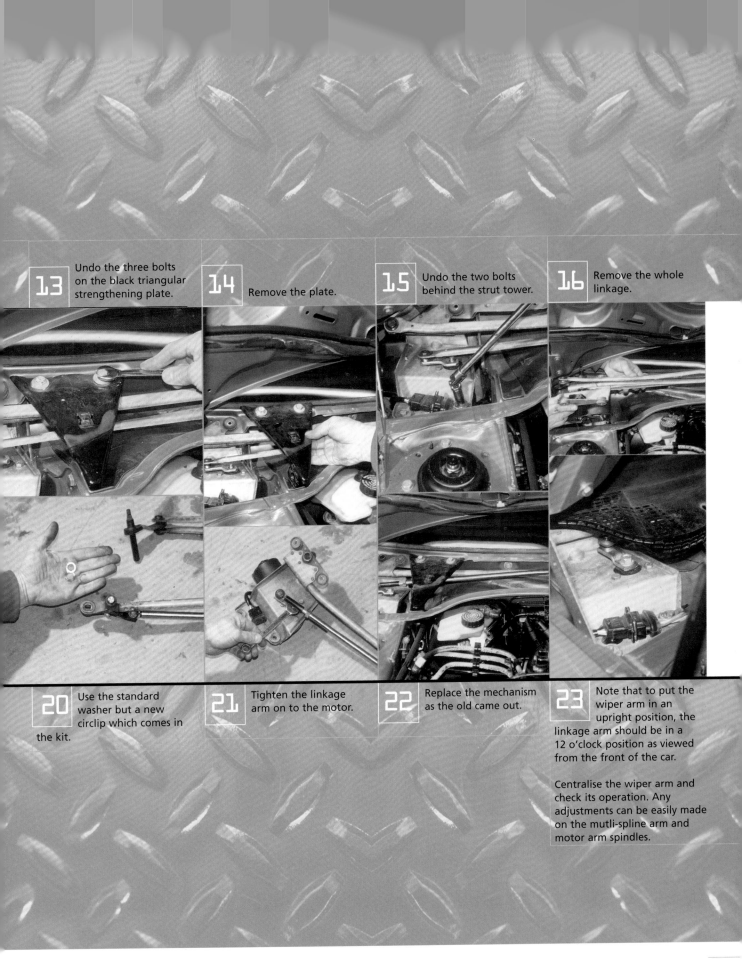

13 Undo the three bolts on the black triangular strengthening plate.

14 Remove the plate.

15 Undo the two bolts behind the strut tower.

16 Remove the whole linkage.

20 Use the standard washer but a new circlip which comes in the kit.

21 Tighten the linkage arm on to the motor.

22 Replace the mechanism as the old came out.

23 Note that to put the wiper arm in an upright position, the linkage arm should be in a 12 o'clock position as viewed from the front of the car.

Centralise the wiper arm and check its operation. Any adjustments can be easily made on the mutli-spline arm and motor arm spindles.

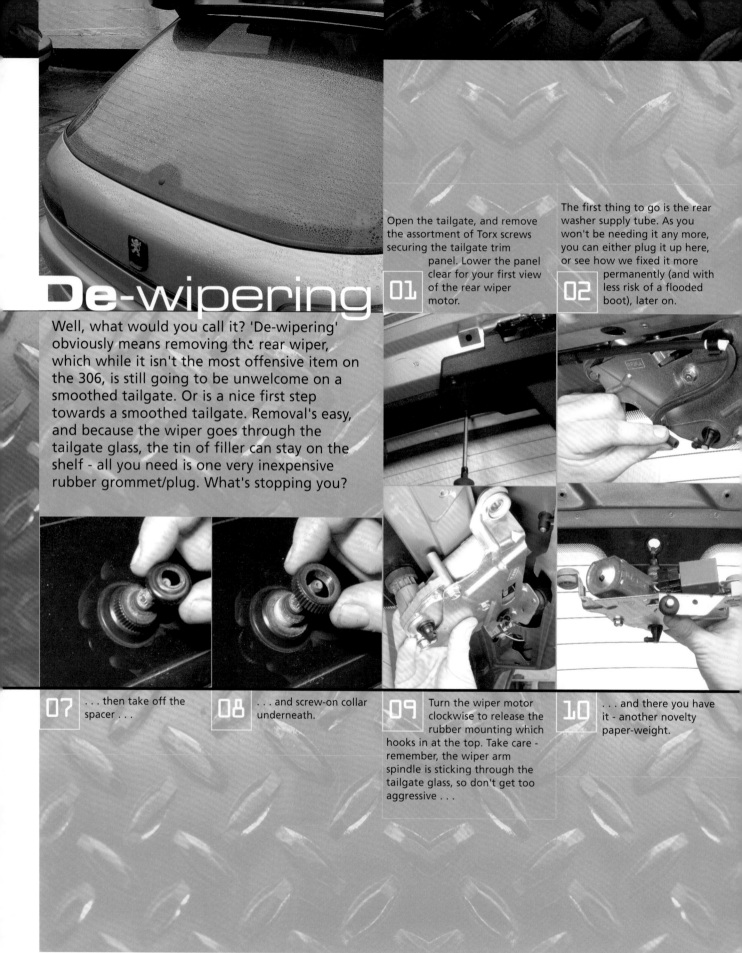

De-wipering

Well, what would you call it? 'De-wipering' obviously means removing the rear wiper, which while it isn't the most offensive item on the 306, is still going to be unwelcome on a smoothed tailgate. Or is a nice first step towards a smoothed tailgate. Removal's easy, and because the wiper goes through the tailgate glass, the tin of filler can stay on the shelf - all you need is one very inexpensive rubber grommet/plug. What's stopping you?

01 Open the tailgate, and remove the assortment of Torx screws securing the tailgate trim panel. Lower the panel clear for your first view of the rear wiper motor.

02 The first thing to go is the rear washer supply tube. As you won't be needing it any more, you can either plug it up here, or see how we fixed it more permanently (and with less risk of a flooded boot), later on.

07 . . . then take off the spacer . . .

08 . . . and screw-on collar underneath.

09 Turn the wiper motor clockwise to release the rubber mounting which hooks in at the top. Take care - remember, the wiper arm spindle is sticking through the tailgate glass, so don't get too aggressive . . .

10 . . . and there you have it - another novelty paper-weight.

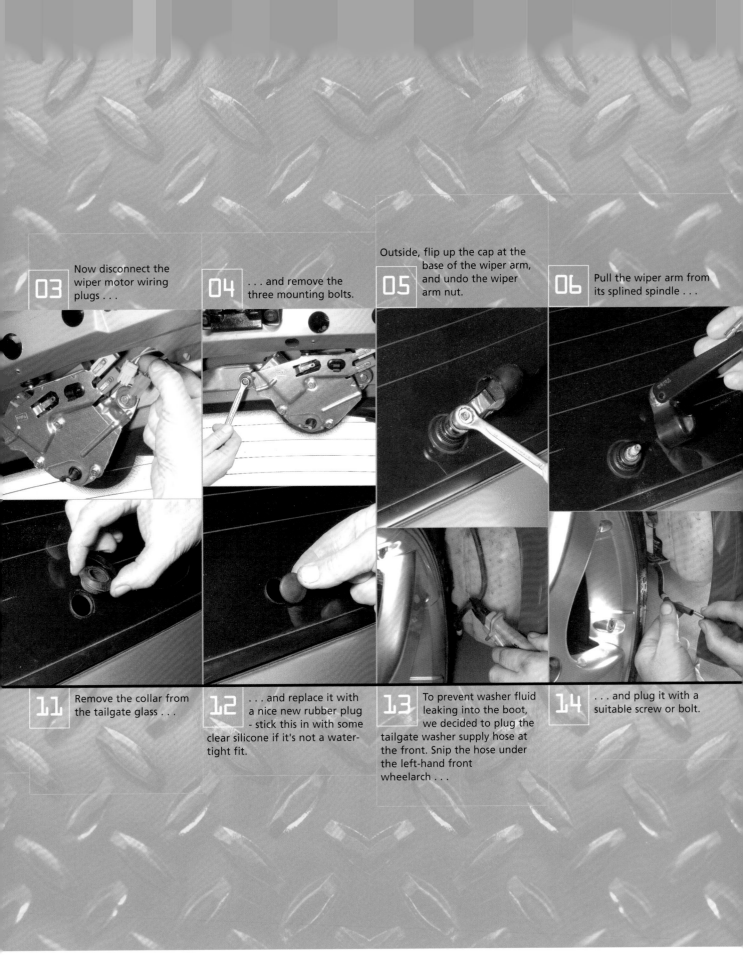

03 Now disconnect the wiper motor wiring plugs . . .

04 . . . and remove the three mounting bolts.

05 Outside, flip up the cap at the base of the wiper arm, and undo the wiper arm nut.

06 Pull the wiper arm from its splined spindle . . .

11 Remove the collar from the tailgate glass . . .

12 . . . and replace it with a nice new rubber plug - stick this in with some clear silicone if it's not a water-tight fit.

13 To prevent washer fluid leaking into the boot, we decided to plug the tailgate washer supply hose at the front. Snip the hose under the left-hand front wheelarch . . .

14 . . . and plug it with a suitable screw or bolt.

The standard Peugeot cap is matched on the other side of the car so doesn't look too bad, but it could look better with a performance part.

Fuel filler cap

If your goal is making your car stand out from the crowd, going that little bit further in the work involved can make all the difference in the way it'll be viewed. Case in point? The fuel filler cap, of which there are many 'stick-on lookalikes' that do nothing for the car and even less for your credibility. The filler cap we've chosen is a proper aero-style cap which is far more involved to fit than any other type, but it's worth it for the finished appearance. In fact, if you're worried about tackling bodywork we'd go so far as to say don't start the job, because it does take a bit of experience to finish well. If you're prepared to give it a go however, you can take it so far and have a bodyshop at least do the final filling and paint, which is required to get the finish top notch anyway.

05 Remove the press-in plastic plugs with a screwdriver, but be gentle because they break easily.

02 The kit comes with the aluminium cap, an aluminium surround/housing, cork gasket, resin composite plug and a tube of sealer.

03 To remove the standard cap pop it open first, whereby you should be able to see where it bolts through the bodywork via a hinged bracket.

04 To get to the nuts which hold the filler cap bracket in place, you first need to remove the plastic arch liner. Undo the front bolt holding this in place.

06 Remove the plastic arch liner. You can now reach up behind the bodywork with a 10mm spanner and undo the filler cap hinge bracket's nuts.

07 In the filler cap hole, remove the locating grommets top and bottom.

08 Unscrew and, from the back of the bodywork accessed via the wheelarch, remove the door release mechanism. This is on a cable going through to the driver's footwell, so cut the cable off where it enters the bodywork.

09 You should now be left with the hole plus the filler cap, which has to be removed also.

10 Fit the resin plug and note that the hole goes towards the rear edge. It should fit flush, but ours didn't.

11 A Dremel multi tool is handy to remove excess material on the back, but do it bit by bit and keep rechecking the fit.

12 While checking the fit, it's useful to mark the position of the plug accurately with a pen so it slots back in the same place each time you check it.

17 The glass-fibre reinforced resin is Isopon's P40, while on the right the black sealer comes with the kit.

18 Spread the sealer on the rear of the plug which sits against the fuel filler neck. Mix up the resin at this point too.

13 When the fit is right, remove the plug and grind grooves all around the edge of the hole. These help locate the plug by giving the fixing resin something to grip on.

14 Remove the paint from the inner edge of the hole.

15 Remove the paint from at least two inches all the way around the hole. It's best if a cover is fitted over the fuel filler neck.

16 Prepare the back of the plug and its edge with 80-grit sandpaper, so the resin grips well to it.

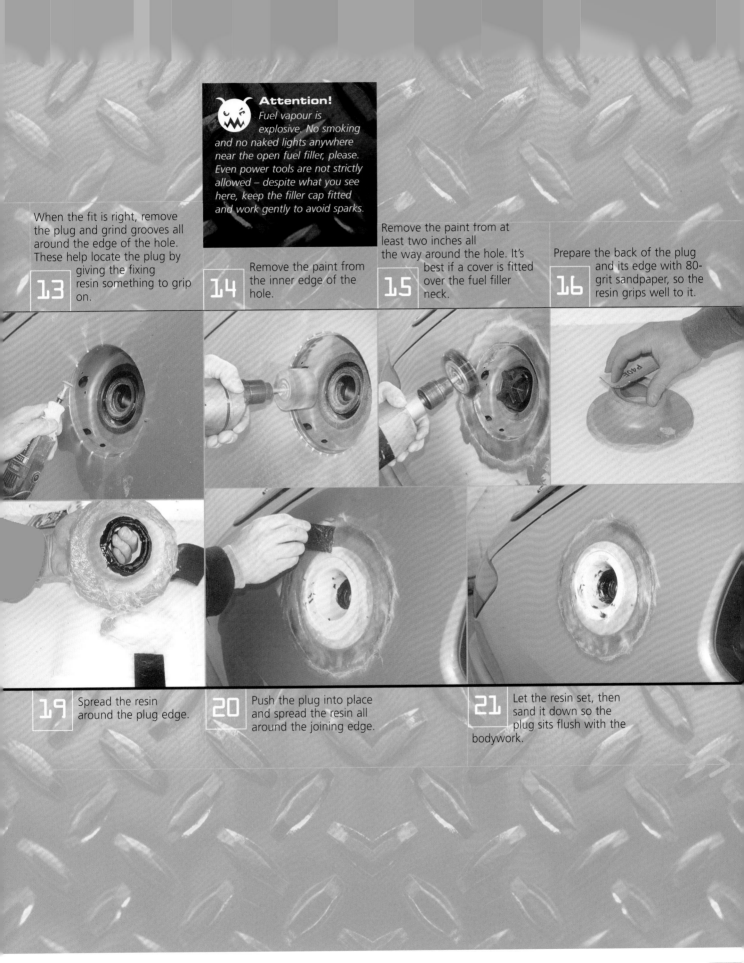

19 Spread the resin around the plug edge.

20 Push the plug into place and spread the resin all around the joining edge.

21 Let the resin set, then sand it down so the plug sits flush with the bodywork.

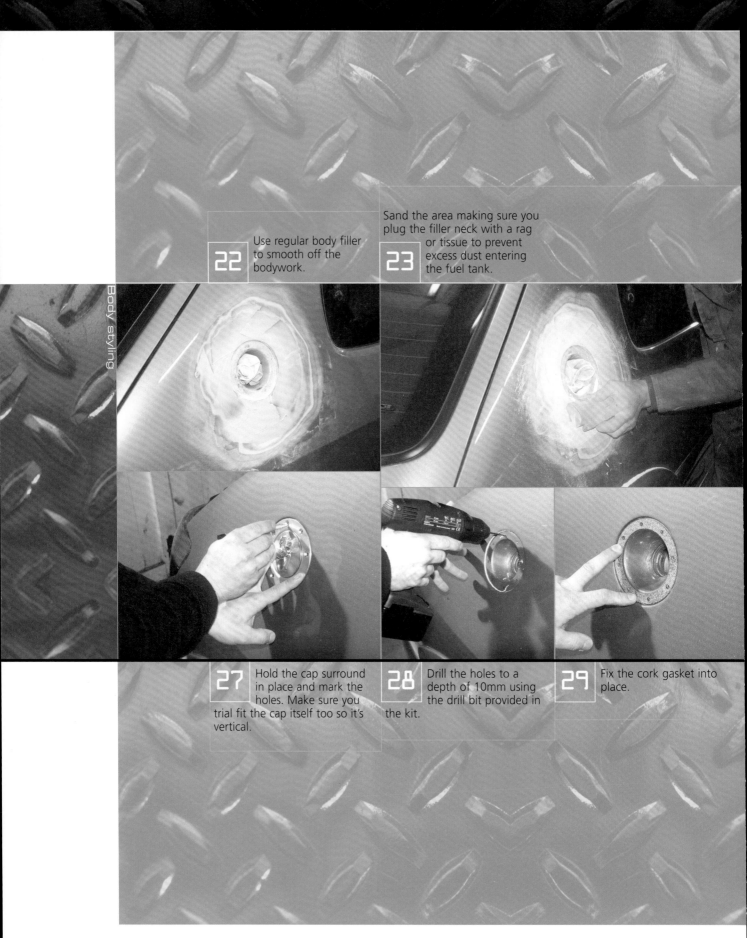

22 Use regular body filler to smooth off the bodywork.

23 Sand the area making sure you plug the filler neck with a rag or tissue to prevent excess dust entering the fuel tank.

27 Hold the cap surround in place and mark the holes. Make sure you trial fit the cap itself too so it's vertical.

28 Drill the holes to a depth of 10mm using the drill bit provided in the kit.

29 Fix the cork gasket into place.

24 Spray the area with filler/primer, then once dry flat it back.

25 Spray on the coats of body colour and, once dry, flat it back and spray on the lacquer

26 The finished job should look smooth and the hole should appear like it's always been there.

30 Fit the housing using the Torx screws and key provided

31 The finished housing should now be ready for the cap - the finished job looks every bit the motorsport part it is.

Rear spoiler

Rear spoilers on road cars do little to provide actual downforce. What they can achieve, however, is a redirection of airflow to keep your rear screen clean, plus they can reduce the air turbulence behind a car, thus meaning there's less drag, allowing your car a slight increase in top speed. The smaller spoilers are, usually the more ineffective they are, so swapping the standard item on a 306 for one such as the Ecosse rear spoiler, can make a whole heap of difference.

The Ecosse version not only improves the airflow, it looks damn fine while doing it. It brings some shape to the back of the car, which is otherwise just a rounded fat rear without enough character. Whether or not you have the rest of the Ecosse bodykit doesn't matter, that can be done at a later date because the spoiler looks good by itself.

The minor job of wire connections on the spoiler is easily handled, but the main part of the job is actually routing the wires in the first place. Give yourself at least a day to do the job, once the spoiler has been painted.

The 306 XSi standard spoiler is designed to blend in with the rear window so it doesn't spoil the car's lines. Time to change that!

01

02 The Ecosse roof spoiler is radical in design plus, handily, its fits where the old one does (though needs a couple more holes in the hatch frame). It also incorporates a third (or in this case fourth!) brake light.

03 First stop for the roof spoiler should be the spray shop, to match whatever body colour your car is.

04 After a light sanding with 800-grit paper, the spoiler can be primered then guide coated and filled wherever any low points show up after sanding.

05 Once the colour goes on the spoiler will need flatting down prior to the lacquer coat.

>>

06 With the new spoiler ready, you can remove the old one which is bolted through the rear screen.

07 Undo the four bolts all the way along the glass, being careful not to slip onto the screen.

08 The spoiler can now be removed.

12 The extra brake light comes with its own wiring loom and connectors to tie it into the brake light system.

13 Connect the plug of the loom into the rear of the additional brake light.

14 Push the other end of the loom though the hole behind the brake light.

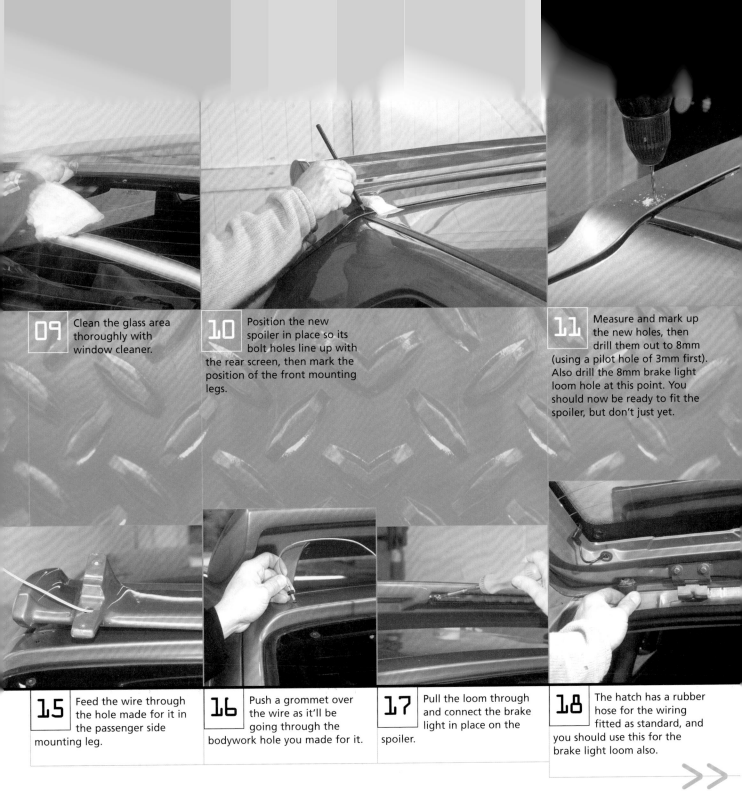

09 Clean the glass area thoroughly with window cleaner.

10 Position the new spoiler in place so its bolt holes line up with the rear screen, then mark the position of the front mounting legs.

11 Measure and mark up the new holes, then drill them out to 8mm (using a pilot hole of 3mm first). Also drill the 8mm brake light loom hole at this point. You should now be ready to fit the spoiler, but don't just yet.

15 Feed the wire through the hole made for it in the passenger side mounting leg.

16 Push a grommet over the wire as it'll be going through the bodywork hole you made for it.

17 Pull the loom through and connect the brake light in place on the spoiler.

18 The hatch has a rubber hose for the wiring fitted as standard, and you should use this for the brake light loom also.

>>

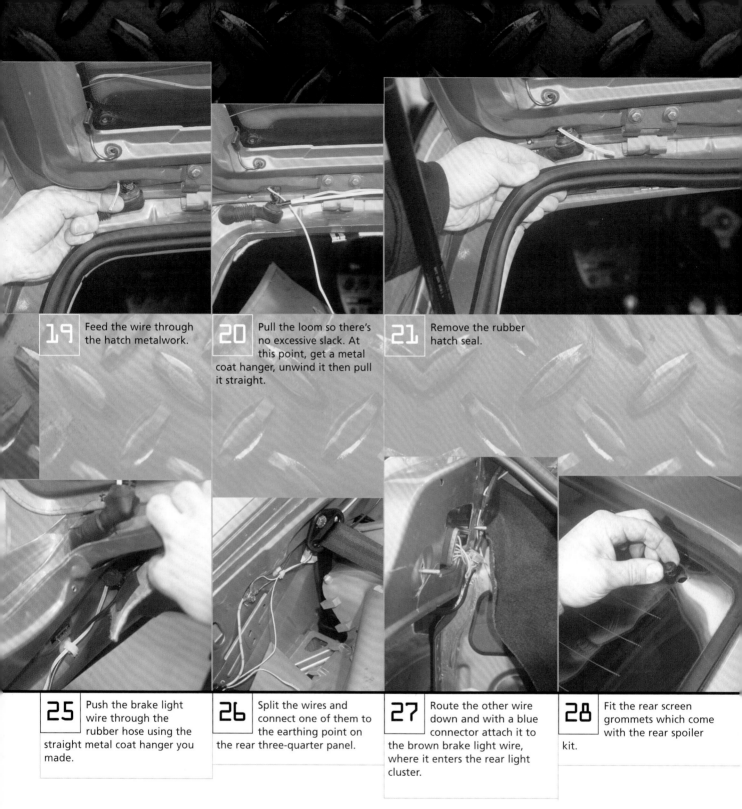

19 Feed the wire through the hatch metalwork.

20 Pull the loom so there's no excessive slack. At this point, get a metal coat hanger, unwind it then pull it straight.

21 Remove the rubber hatch seal.

25 Push the brake light wire through the rubber hose using the straight metal coat hanger you made.

26 Split the wires and connect one of them to the earthing point on the rear three-quarter panel.

27 Route the other wire down and with a blue connector attach it to the brown brake light wire, where it enters the rear light cluster.

28 Fit the rear screen grommets which come with the rear spoiler kit.

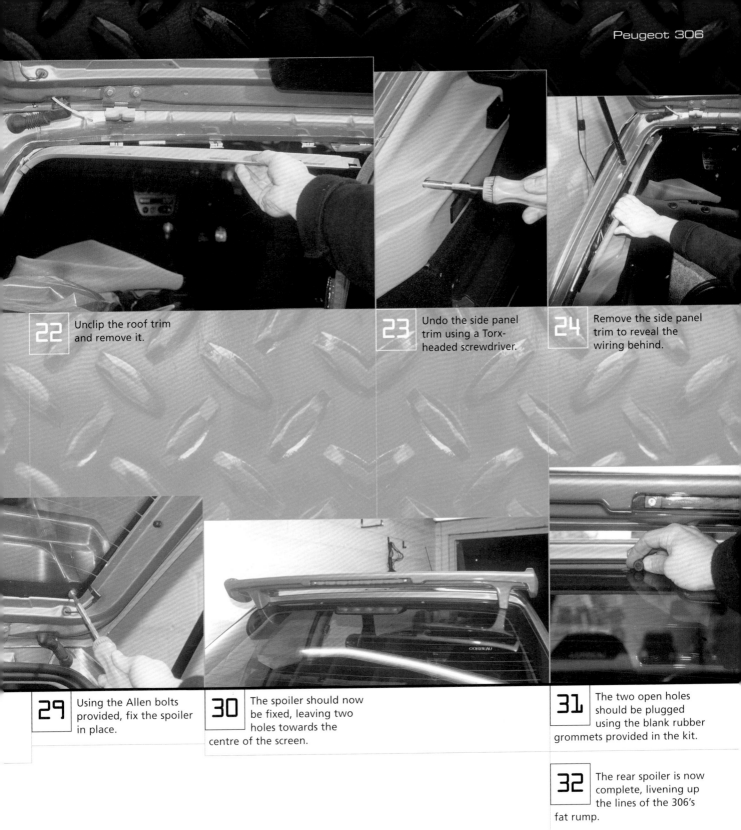

22 Unclip the roof trim and remove it.

23 Undo the side panel trim using a Torx-headed screwdriver.

24 Remove the side panel trim to reveal the wiring behind.

29 Using the Allen bolts provided, fix the spoiler in place.

30 The spoiler should now be fixed, leaving two holes towards the centre of the screen.

31 The two open holes should be plugged using the blank rubber grommets provided in the kit.

32 The rear spoiler is now complete, livening up the lines of the 306's fat rump.

With the headlights, full beam and fog lights on you'll have enough wattage to light up Wembley.

Front bumper

Body styling

The Peugeot Ecosse Mygale body kit is comprehensive and of fine quality. It has front and rear bumpers to replace the original items, combined side skirts and rear three-quarter panels plus a roof spoiler which again replaces the original part.

A well designed body kit should always use the original car's mounts for the new parts, as it reduces the areas that can go wrong during fitting. However, some standard fittings are surplus to aftermarket requirements, after all if you smack your front or rear bumper against a wall, for instance, an extra bracket isn't going to save it, it'll just bend or pull away from its mounting point and create more damage. Hence, the Mygale kit uses the minimum bolt-on points to make it secure and fairly simple to fit.

Now, you could spray these parts yourself, but we wouldn't recommend it because the finish you're likely to get will not be up to factory standards. So, it's worth visiting a bodyshop to get a quote for spraying the body kit, before you start fitting it (which isn't too tricky). That way you can at least work to a set budget.

01 The standard XSi bumper incorporates foglamps and is a good looking piece, though is a bit too shallow and rounded to appear aggressive.

02 To remove the bumper, first jack the car up and place it on stands. Undo the three 10mm bolts along its base.

R580 PVC

> **03** The inner arch liner has to be removed in order to get the mounting bolts, so remove the screws underneath first.

04 Undo the screws within the arch next. These are often clogged up with dirt, so clean them out using a small screwdriver.

05 You can now remove the front bumper's plastic splash guard.

06 You have to take out the inner arch liner next, which means prising out the poppers.

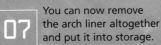

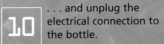

07 You can now remove the arch liner altogether and put it into storage.

08 The front bumper bolt is behind the washer bottle, so this also needs to be removed . . .

09 . . . to do this you first have to unscrew the washer bottle filler neck . . .

10 . . . and unplug the electrical connection to the bottle.

>>

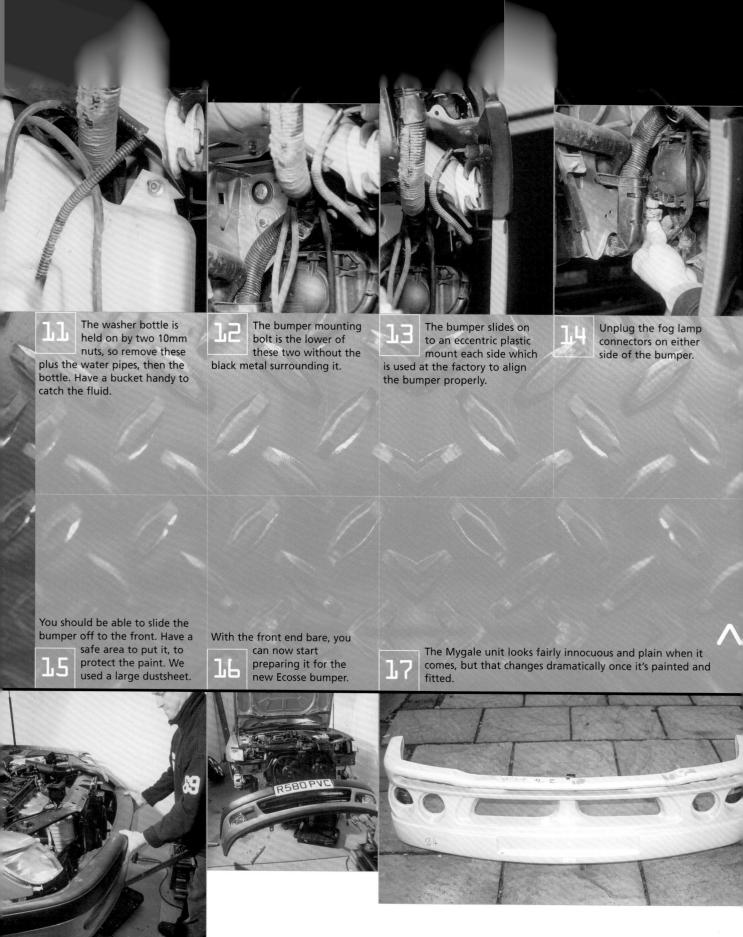

11 The washer bottle is held on by two 10mm nuts, so remove these plus the water pipes, then the bottle. Have a bucket handy to catch the fluid.

12 The bumper mounting bolt is the lower of these two without the black metal surrounding it.

13 The bumper slides on to an eccentric plastic mount each side which is used at the factory to align the bumper properly.

14 Unplug the fog lamp connectors on either side of the bumper.

15 You should be able to slide the bumper off to the front. Have a safe area to put it, to protect the paint. We used a large dustsheet.

16 With the front end bare, you can now start preparing it for the new Ecosse bumper.

17 The Mygale unit looks fairly innocuous and plain when it comes, but that changes dramatically once it's painted and fitted.

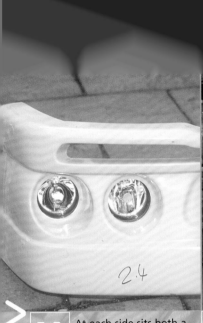

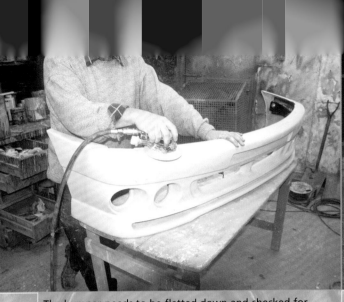

18 At each side sits both a fog light (the inner one), plus a spotlight which should be linked up to the main beam.

19 The bumper needs to be flatted down and checked for any blemishes prior to primering.

20 Use a filler primer to even out the surface and make it completely smooth.

21 A guide coat is essential in making sure you've picked up on any small imperfections.

22 Flat the bumper back again and fill any low spots as necessary, then it's ready for the colour coat.

23 Spray on the colour coat and flat back the finish with 1200-grit paper between coats, then add the lacquer top coat.

24 The eccentric bumper mounts aren't used on the Ecosse bumper, so these need to be removed.

>>

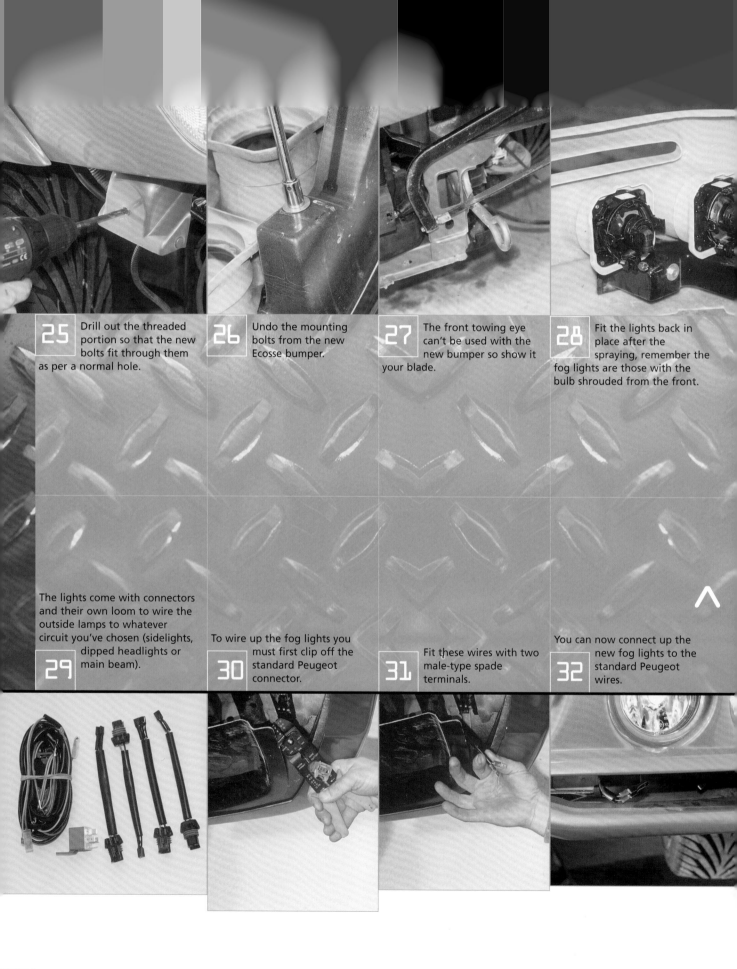

25 Drill out the threaded portion so that the new bolts fit through them as per a normal hole.

26 Undo the mounting bolts from the new Ecosse bumper.

27 The front towing eye can't be used with the new bumper so show it your blade.

28 Fit the lights back in place after the spraying, remember the fog lights are those with the bulb shrouded from the front.

29 The lights come with connectors and their own loom to wire the outside lamps to whatever circuit you've chosen (sidelights, dipped headlights or main beam).

30 To wire up the fog lights you must first clip off the standard Peugeot connector.

31 Fit these wires with two male-type spade terminals.

32 You can now connect up the new fog lights to the standard Peugeot wires.

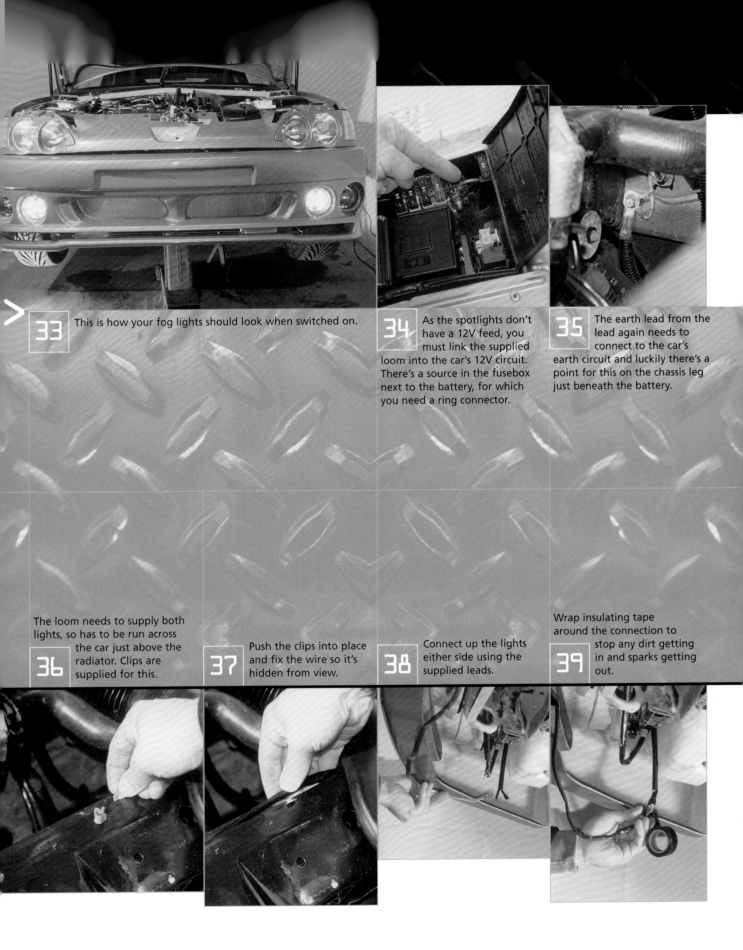

33 This is how your fog lights should look when switched on.

34 As the spotlights don't have a 12V feed, you must link the supplied loom into the car's 12V circuit. There's a source in the fusebox next to the battery, for which you need a ring connector.

35 The earth lead from the lead again needs to connect to the car's earth circuit and luckily there's a point for this on the chassis leg just beneath the battery.

36 The loom needs to supply both lights, so has to be run across the car just above the radiator. Clips are supplied for this.

37 Push the clips into place and fix the wire so it's hidden from view.

38 Connect up the lights either side using the supplied leads.

39 Wrap insulating tape around the connection to stop any dirt getting in and sparks getting out.

Rear bumper

The Mygale rear bumper comes as part of the Peugeot Ecosse package and isn't really any good alone. It's a deep piece which breaks up the overly rounded rear lines of the 306's body, flaring outwards towards the wheels which will no doubt be wider if you've come this far.

Though the standard 306 XSi has a hidden exhaust, the Mygale rear bumper allows room for up to a 4-inch pipe at a squeeze, though a 3-inch outlet back box sits much more comfortably in there. The bumper also has room for the rear towing eye (unlike the Mygale front bumper), so if you ever break down at least you can tow the car home, err, backwards. It uses the same but fewer mounting points and new lower brackets are supplied with the kit.

Like any parts of a bodykit, you really should have it sprayed by a professional. Reckon on about an eight-hour day to fit the bumper, with an hour for lunch and two 15-minute tea breaks.

01 With neatly rounded lines and very smooth lights, the XSi is hardly ugly, but it does lack a performance feel, especially with no exhaust showing.

02 To start the job, take off the rear light cluster cover inside the boot. This is held on by two hand-tight wing nuts.

R580 PVC

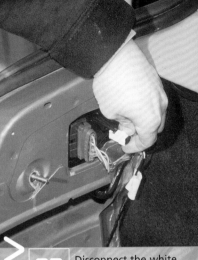

03 Disconnect the white numberplate light connector from the passenger side rear light cluster.

04 Jack the rear of the car up, place it on axle stands and get underneath. To the side, just behind the rear arch you'll see a square hole each side with insulation showing though. Push the insulation back to reveal the bumper mounting bolt.

05 More mounting bolts are accessed from the inside the boot, along the lower rear edge.

06 The last bolts to remove are the ones from underneath.

07 Finally, there's the screws to the arch liner which need to be removed.

08 You can remove the whole bumper, but make sure the wiring for the numberplate comes through the bodywork grommet okay.

09 The 306's bare bum can then be cleaned ready to take the new Ecosse version of bumper.

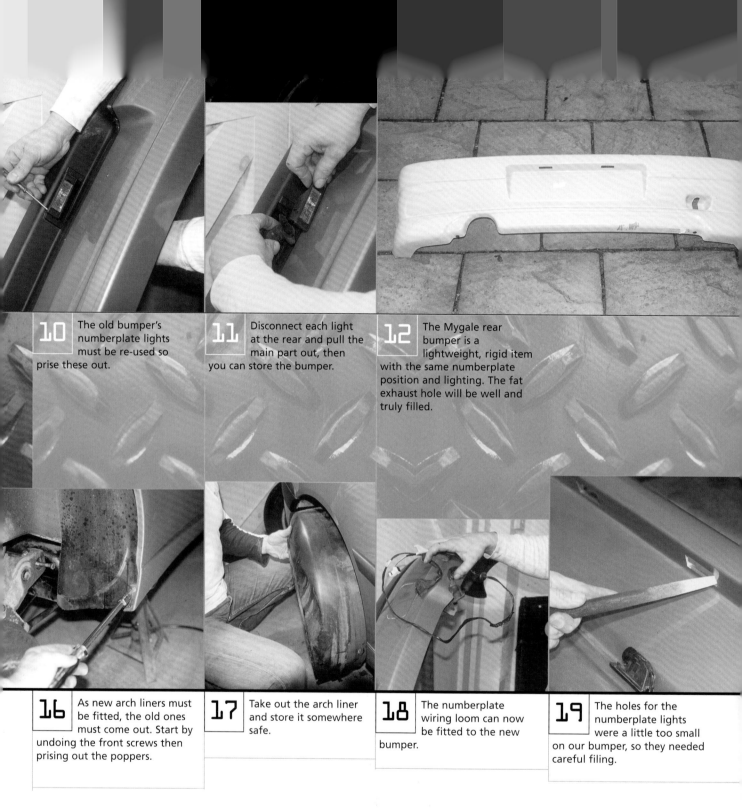

10 The old bumper's numberplate lights must be re-used so prise these out.

11 Disconnect each light at the rear and pull the main part out, then you can store the bumper.

12 The Mygale rear bumper is a lightweight, rigid item with the same numberplate position and lighting. The fat exhaust hole will be well and truly filled.

16 As new arch liners must be fitted, the old ones must come out. Start by undoing the front screws then prising out the poppers.

17 Take out the arch liner and store it somewhere safe.

18 The numberplate wiring loom can now be fitted to the new bumper.

19 The holes for the numberplate lights were a little too small on our bumper, so they needed careful filing.

13 After flatting down and primering, give the bumper a guide coat to reveal any blemishes while sanding.

14 Have the colour coats sprayed on and flat the surface down between coats, then lacquer the bumper to finish it.

15 The mounting points have new brackets supplied and fitted already to the bumper.

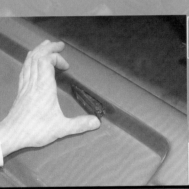

20 Push the lights into place making sure they're not too loose.

21 The lights should fit flush as per the standard car.

22 Connect the wiring loom to the back of the lights.

23 Push the white connector through the original hole and plug it back into the light cluster.

24 Fit the bumper on to the original mounts and you're done. How much better does that look?

Side skirts/arches

Front and rear bodykit bumpers may make a car look better, but unless the lines are further complemented by deep side skirts, the ground effect will be lost. The Peugeot Ecosse Mygale bodykit comes with more than just a pair of side skirts too, as the skirt extends both the arches and fills out the rear three-quarter panel to bulk out the 306's otherwise slab sides.

The kit comes from France via Scotland, so has a long journey and our first set of skirts had suffered for it. A broken rear arch on one side meant a new side skirt had to be ordered, so be careful to check your delivery before signing for it.

Moulded into the rear of the skirts are bolts which go through the bodywork. These have washers plus lock nuts (also supplied) fixed to the other side. In the case of the rear three-quarter panel these are hard to get to, requiring the removal of the interior rear panels.

The side skirts come with glass-fibre templates with which to mark out the holes to be drilled, though cleverly they also use the trim holes once the plastic side trims have been removed. The templates must be used while the front and rear bumpers are off, hence the side skirts need to be done at the same time.

New glass-fibre arch liners are supplied front and rear, and can be fitted in the stock positions once the side skirts are on.

01 The 306 not only needs lowering, the overall effect of the car needs to be enhanced by extending the bodywork down.

02 The side skirts come supplied with glass-fibre templates which are used to mark the holes to be drilled around the front and rear arches.

03 Moulded into the rear of the skirts are bolts, some of which use the stock trim holes, saving you fitting time.

04 The process of flatting back, primering, sanding and guide coating are the same as with the rest of the bodykit.

05 The finished skirts, prior to lacquering. Time to get the body prepped.

06 The rear trim slides forward and unclips with a bit of force. The dirtier and older they are, the more difficult they become to remove.

07 Some of the clips might well break off from the trim in the process, but just pull these out with pliers.

08 The front trim just under the indicator also needs to be removed. If the arch liner is out you can get a hand to the back, which helps.

09 The templates supplied fit into the trim holes and snug around the arch.

>>

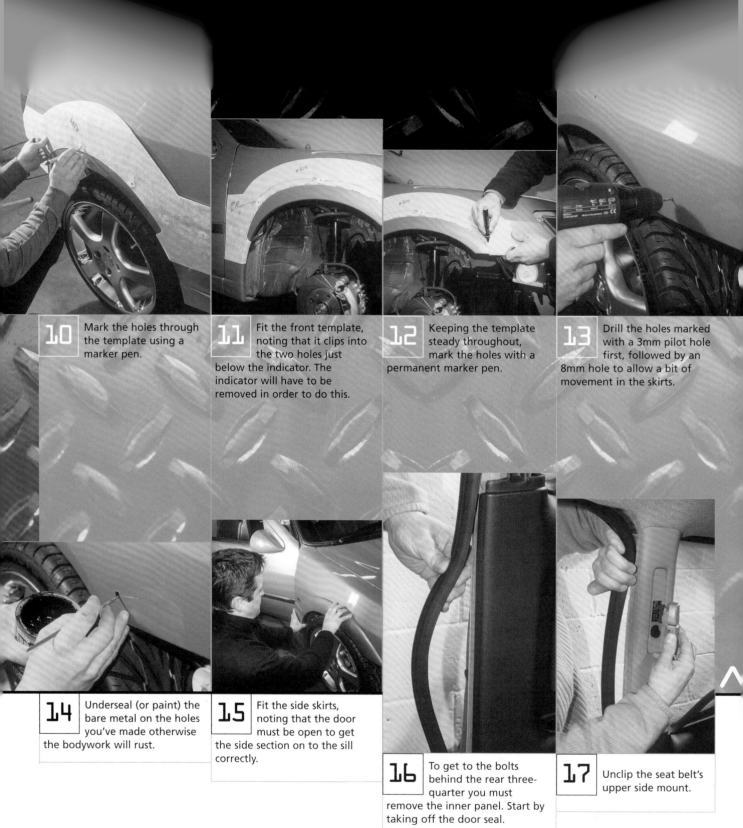

10 Mark the holes through the template using a marker pen.

11 Fit the front template, noting that it clips into the two holes just below the indicator. The indicator will have to be removed in order to do this.

12 Keeping the template steady throughout, mark the holes with a permanent marker pen.

13 Drill the holes marked with a 3mm pilot hole first, followed by an 8mm hole to allow a bit of movement in the skirts.

14 Underseal (or paint) the bare metal on the holes you've made otherwise the bodywork will rust.

15 Fit the side skirts, noting that the door must be open to get the side section on to the sill correctly.

16 To get to the bolts behind the rear three-quarter you must remove the inner panel. Start by taking off the door seal.

17 Unclip the seat belt's upper side mount.

18 Prise off the door pillar trim by hand and the inner panel can then be pulled back enough to get behind.

19 Using the washers and locking nuts supplied, tighten the side skirts against the body.

20 The new Ecosse glass-fibre arches can go in once the side skirts have been fixed in place.

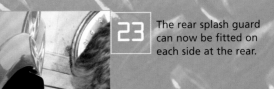

23 The rear splash guard can now be fitted on each side at the rear.

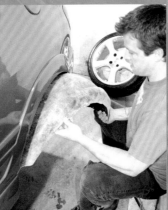

The finished skirts follow the lines of the front and rear bumpers perfectly. The door side trim should be colour coded so it doesn't stand out as here.

24

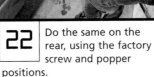

21 Push them into place, taking care not to scratch the arches. A strip of masking tape to protect the arch lip would help here.

22 Do the same on the rear, using the factory screw and popper positions.

De-locking

One very popular way to tidy up the 306 lines is to do away with the (frankly ugly) door locks. With no lock barrels to attack, this also defeats another way into the car for thieves. Most owners of 3-door 306s don't mess with the door handles - removing and flushing the rear door handles (on 5-door models) is okay, legally/MOT-speaking, but removing the front door handles completely will land you in trouble, come MOT time. Still, there's no harm in removing them temporarily, to colour-code them...

First, the door trim panel has to come off - but you knew that already. Look in "Window tinting", for door trim panel removal. Reach inside the door, and undo the nut securing the metal plate inside the door handle . . .

01

02 . . . take out the plate . . .

07 Meanwhile, back at the lock barrel. Use a screwdriver to push the barrel's horseshoe-shaped retaining clip forwards . . .

08 . . . and then take it out of the door. The lock barrel should by now have fallen out. Unclip and remove the lock barrel operating rod.

09 Now to get rid of the rather unsightly hole you've just created. Our method was to glue a piece of bumper mesh inside first, to support the filler. Mix up the epoxy glue, apply to your piece of mesh . . .

10 . . . and stick it in the door.

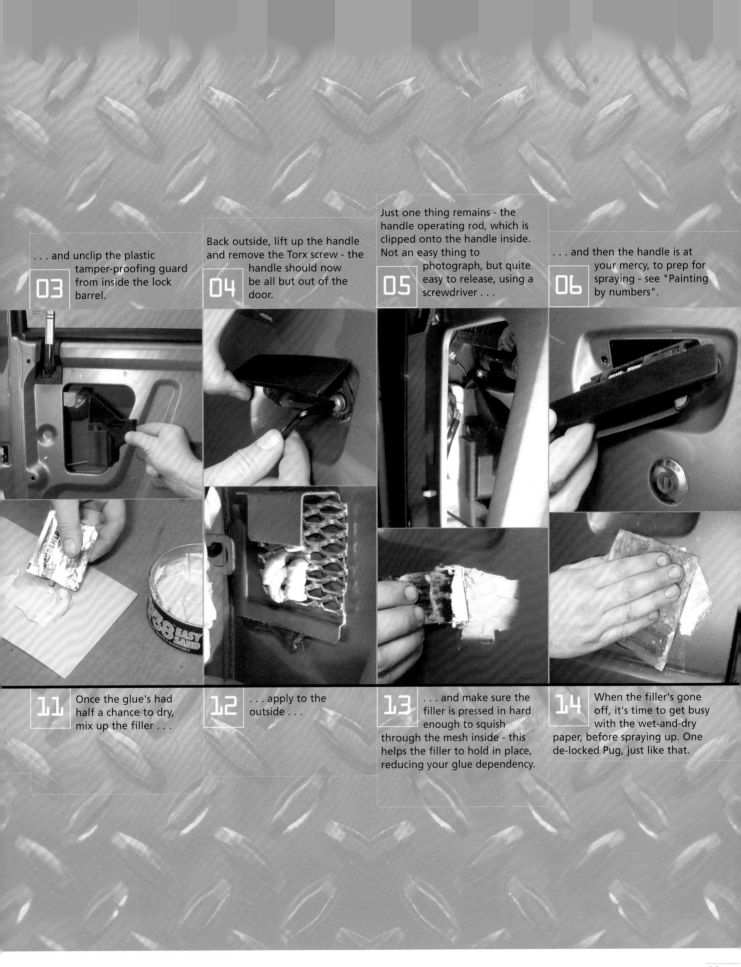

03 . . . and unclip the plastic tamper-proofing guard from inside the lock barrel.

04 Back outside, lift up the handle and remove the Torx screw - the handle should now be all but out of the door.

05 Just one thing remains - the handle operating rod, which is clipped onto the handle inside. Not an easy thing to photograph, but quite easy to release, using a screwdriver . . .

06 . . . and then the handle is at your mercy, to prep for spraying - see "Painting by numbers".

11 Once the glue's had half a chance to dry, mix up the filler . . .

12 . . . apply to the outside . . .

13 . . . and make sure the filler is pressed in hard enough to squish through the mesh inside - this helps the filler to hold in place, reducing your glue dependency.

14 When the filler's gone off, it's time to get busy with the wet-and-dry paper, before spraying up. One de-locked Pug, just like that.

Remote locking

Virtually all 306s except the real basic models have central locking, and the posher models have remote locking too - bonus! Remote locking kits are available from several Peugeot parts suppliers, or you can buy a locking extension module for most aftermarket alarms.

To wire up your alarm interface, the best advice is to follow the instructions with the kit - it's impossible to second-guess detailed instructions like this. The standard central locking control module is under the carpet below the driver's seat. One piece of advice to bear in mind when tracking down the locking trigger wires is not to disconnect the wiring plugs, for testing - the locking system won't work at all if you do, and you won't learn anything. Peugeot wiring is a bit more mysterious than most, and relies on wire numbers rather than colours - dare we suggest the Haynes manual wiring diagrams? On most 306s, the wire numbers you're after are 620 (red) and 621 (yellow) for the lock and unlock trigger wires. Good luck!

When you come to test the operation, first make sure at least one window's open, in the unlikely event you lock yourself out. Also check that the doors are locked when the alarm's armed, and not the other way round.

Tricks 'n' tips

If your battery goes flat, you'll be locked out. We ran two thin wires from the battery terminals (with a 10-amp fuse in the live, and the ends insulated), and tucked them away for access from below in an emergency. By connecting a slave battery to these wires (do not try jump-starting), you'll put enough juice into the system to operate the locks, saving you a red face. Think it over.

Bonnet vents

Once you've got your bodykit on, it's only natural you'll want a bonnet vent, isn't it? Respect. But this is one scary job to tackle yourself, unless you're really that good, or that brave. Leave it in the hands of the professionals, is our advice. Plenty of options - you can get little louvres stamped in as well, to complement your Evo, Impreza, Integrale or Celica GT4 main vent. There's even people using the bonnet scoop from a Kia Sedona people carrier! Truly, anything goes.

Being scene

Lights - one of the easiest and coolest ways to trick up your Pug. Several options here, so we'll start at the front, and work back.

Lights
& bulbs

Headlights

Almost nothing influences the look of your 306 more than the front end, so the headlights play a crucial role.

What's available?

For most people, there's essentially three popular routes to modding the 306 headlights - two cheap, and one rather less cheap (but more effective).

The popular cheap option is stick-on headlight "brows", which do give the attractive but not-all-that-hard front end a tougher look. The brows are best sprayed to match the car, before fitting - some have sticky pads, others can be fitted using mastic.

Another cheap option is again stick-on - this time, it's stick-on covers which give the twin-headlight look. This is basically a sheet of vinyl (shaped to the headlights, and colour-matched to your car) with two holes cut in it. Dead easy to fit, but a bit of a style no-no.

Getting more expensive, we're looking at complete replacement twin lights, which can be sourced from Peugeot themselves, besides the long-standing favourites from Morette. When you're buying any lights, make sure they're UK-legal - they must be E-marked, and for right-hand-drive (any advertised as LHD will cause you trouble at MOT time, because the dipped beam pattern will be wrong).

"Proper" twin-headlights deserve proper respect, and come as a complete kit, with separate indicators if you need 'em - facelifted 306s from April 1997-on had lights with built-in winkers. Typically around £300 a set for Morettes at time of writing, these are by no means cheap. The light surrounds have to be sprayed to match your car, and fitting is not without some difficulties, but the finished result is majorly worth it. If you're splashing out on a mean bodykit with front fog/spot light opportunities, you really can't be seen with less than Morettes. Our bodykit came fully equipped with the extra lights - see "Body styling" for wiring-up these babies, in the front bumper section.

Did you know?

The popular twin-headlight look was derived from a cunning tweak first employed in the Touring Cars, years ago. Some teams homologated a twin-headlight unit, but for racing, turned one pair of the "headlights" into air inlets, to direct air from the front of the car to brake ducts or into the engine air intakes, as required. Think about it - why else would the touring cars bother with headlight mods? Until recently, there were no night races!

Twin headlamps

Making a car look individual is imperative in getting it noticed when out cruising. Choosing the right components is part of the process, and everyone has their own opinion as to what looks right. However, the opinion of most of the people into modified cars is that standard headlamps are boring, and twin units almost always look better no matter what car they're on. The 306 has pretty swoopy lights as standard, but the twin units look so much more aggressive that it's difficult not to be tempted.

The units we chose are one of the few items that Peugeot produce themselves, hence they're a perfect fit and come with thorough instructions as their own mechanics have to fit them. The job is quite involved as there's some wiring to do plus a fair bit of dismantling around the front end. However, don't be afraid to tackle it as the job's main drag is the time involved in stripping bits apart.

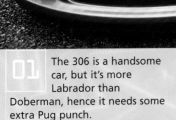

01 The 306 is a handsome car, but it's more Labrador than Doberman, hence it needs some extra Pug punch.

02 The twin headlamp set from Peugeot is an excellent piece of kit which you'll have no problems with.

03 The kit comes with separate indicators as these are normally incorporated in the standard headlamp.

04 Open the bonnet and disconnect the battery, then pop out the four fixing grommets on the front grille. On earlier models, there are screws along the top edge.

05 Undo the bolt holding the grille at the front. Earlier models have screws, accessed through the grille slats.

06 Pull out the strips from beneath the headlamps. The fixings here are tricky to deal with and you might end up breaking some, but these strips won't be re-used afterwards.

07 You can now remove the entire grille.

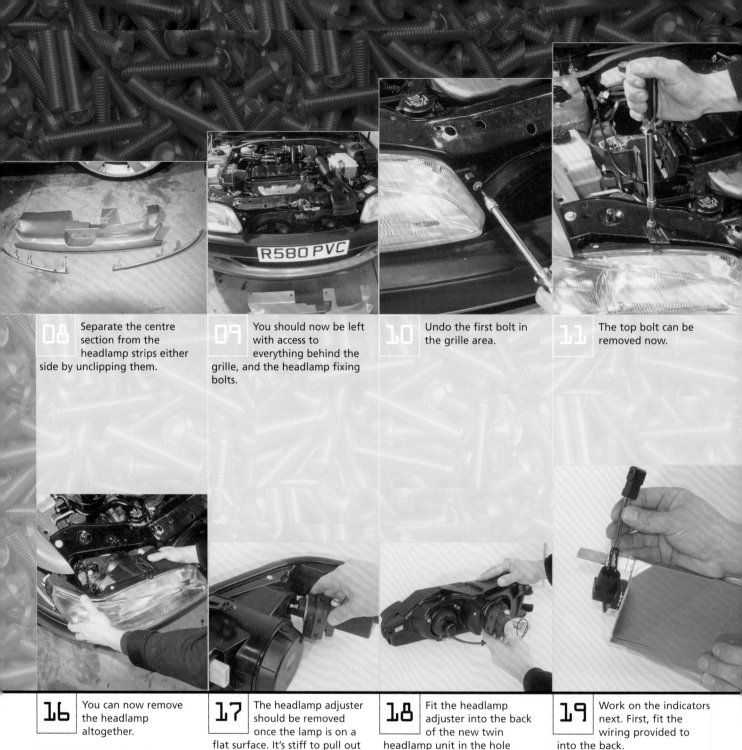

08 Separate the centre section from the headlamp strips either side by unclipping them.

09 You should now be left with access to everything behind the grille, and the headlamp fixing bolts.

10 Undo the first bolt in the grille area.

11 The top bolt can be removed now.

16 You can now remove the headlamp altogether.

17 The headlamp adjuster should be removed once the lamp is on a flat surface. It's stiff to pull out as it's a ball and socket arrangement.

18 Fit the headlamp adjuster into the back of the new twin headlamp unit in the hole provided.

19 Work on the indicators next. First, fit the wiring provided to into the back.

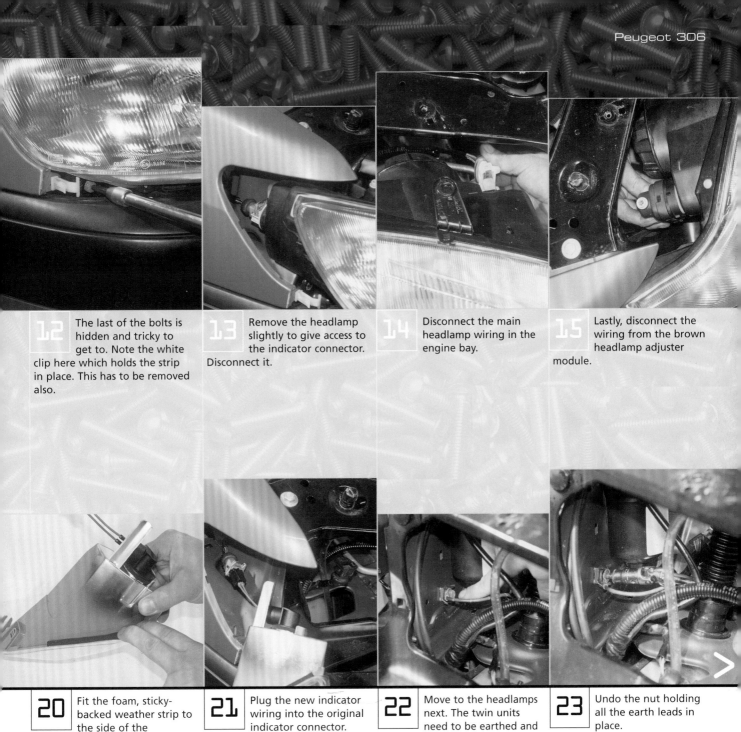

12 The last of the bolts is hidden and tricky to get to. Note the white clip here which holds the strip in place. This has to be removed also.

13 Remove the headlamp slightly to give access to the indicator connector. Disconnect it.

14 Disconnect the main headlamp wiring in the engine bay.

15 Lastly, disconnect the wiring from the brown headlamp adjuster module.

20 Fit the foam, sticky-backed weather strip to the side of the indicator housing as shown. Make sure it's well pushed into place.

21 Plug the new indicator wiring into the original indicator connector.

22 Move to the headlamps next. The twin units need to be earthed and there's a point for this on the offside inner wing and one for the nearside on the chassis leg, just in front of and below the battery.

23 Undo the nut holding all the earth leads in place.

24 Connect the brown earth lead supplied. Note it has a female spade connector end on it.

25 Fit the twin unit in place and secure with all three bolts.

26 If you're sticking with the standard bumper, leaving the housing black has a good look to it as it matches the bumper plastic.

27 The nearside headlamp has all the wiring on it with cables that run across the top of the radiator to the offside unit.

32 Undo the nut and fix the fused live cable supplied in the kit to it.

33 For neatness, route this cable out of the wiring loom hole towards the front of the fuse box, then connect all the loom supplied to both new headlamps.

34 If you're going on to paint the headlamps housings, remove the lamps and unscrew the housing.

35 Pull the housing off the front of the unit.

28 The switch relay is where all the wiring comes from, and it's this which needs to be wired into the car's 12V system.

29 Next to the battery is the main fuse box, which is where you'll get the 12V source from.

30 Open the lid of the fuse box.

31 Inside the box you'll see a 13mm nut positioned at the back.

36 The housing is a single skin piece of ABS plastic, so is pretty resilient.

37 Rub down the housing down with 800-grit wet-and-dry paper.

38 As it's plastic, you need a special primer to spray the housing in preparation for painting.

39 The first coat of gold is on and is being flatted down with 1200-grit wet and dry paper, prior to lacquering.

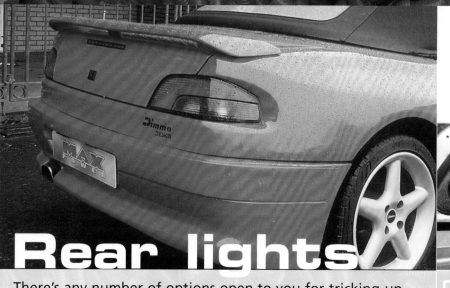

Rear lights

There's any number of options open to you for tricking-up the rear lights - not that the later semi-smoked 306 lights are especially horrible.

When buying rear light clusters, it's not a good idea to go for the cheapest you can find, because you'll be buying trouble. Cheap rear light clusters are usually for left-hand-drive only (typically, they're made for the Euro market, and will only carry TUV approval). The problem concerns rear foglights and rear reflectors, both of which your rear lights must have, to be legal. Mr Plod is too well-informed on this point, and those sexy rear lights are way too big a come-on for him to ignore. Getting around this problem, if your lights aren't legal straight out of the box, is too much grief - only buy UK-legal lights. Period.

New rear clusters for the 306 are a bit pricey, but if you've laid out for Morettes on the front, you might be wanting some Lexus-style clusters at the back. And we salute you. A cheaper option is to colour-code the existing units. Either way, the lights have to come out, and here's how.

01 Open the tailgate, and you'll see two plastic 'wing nuts' holding on the inner covers.

02 Unscrew the nuts . . .

03 . . . and remove the covers. Not too hard, so far. It's worth holding onto the lights as the covers are removed, to avoid giving yourself a fright when they try to fall out.

04 On the left-hand light, there are two wiring plugs to disconnect. The larger brown one has a spring clip holding it in, which you release with a small screwdriver.

05 And out she comes.

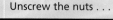

Light tinting

The standard 306 rear lights are far from ugly, but there's no reason not to give 'nature' a helping hand. The easy option with light tinting is to buy the ready-made cans of spray for this purpose, but paint shops have a different method of colour-coding, which might be money well spent.

01 Fist of all, your freshly-removed light must be clean - meths or 'panel wipe' is the only way to be sure that no silicone polish residue remains.

02 You don't want the entire light cluster painted, so get busy with the masking tape.

03 The trick with light-tinting this way is to put the paint on evenly. You'll need more than the suggested two coats to get the lights to really change colour . . .

04 . . . but you'll soon see the effect on the smoked part of the light lens. Obviously, it helps if both rear lights get the same number of coats... Don't go too dark with any colour - Mr Plod won't understand.

05 To see what can be achieved with just light-tinting spray alone, check out the finished result on one of our other project cars, a blue Corsa.

06 And now the professional's version. If you ask a paint shop to colour-code your lights, the effect can be dramatic. For this silver Saxo, the spray was made up of the manufacturer's paint colour, mixed with a lot of lacquer, to make it nearly-transparent. Nice trick - and it looks the business.

M3 side repeaters

At the time of writing this, we actually had great trouble finding pukka replacement side reps that were meant for the 306. So - we thought - what could we fit? Getting creative gives endless possibilities. If you're willing to get brave with the sheet metal, any lights can be made to fit anywhere. Try these M3 side repeaters for size… Quite cheap, too, surprisingly, from our local Beemer dealer.

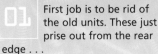

01 First job is to be rid of the old units. These just prise out from the rear edge . . .

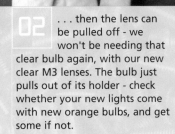

02 . . . then the lens can be pulled off - we won't be needing that clear bulb again, with our new clear M3 lenses. The bulb just pulls out of its holder - check whether your new lights come with new orange bulbs, and get some if not.

07 Time to tidy up the back edge of our new hole with a small file.

08 Now what? The new units still don't fit. A tiny bit more needs to come off at the front edge of our hole, so we mark the required shape with a pen . . .

09 . . . and file out to the mark. At last, the trial fitting is a success.

10 Since we don't want rusty side repeaters, now's a good time to get some paint to those freshly-cut and filed metal edges. You know it makes sense.

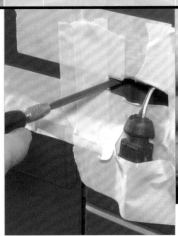

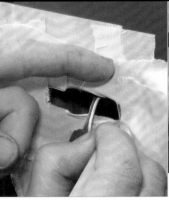

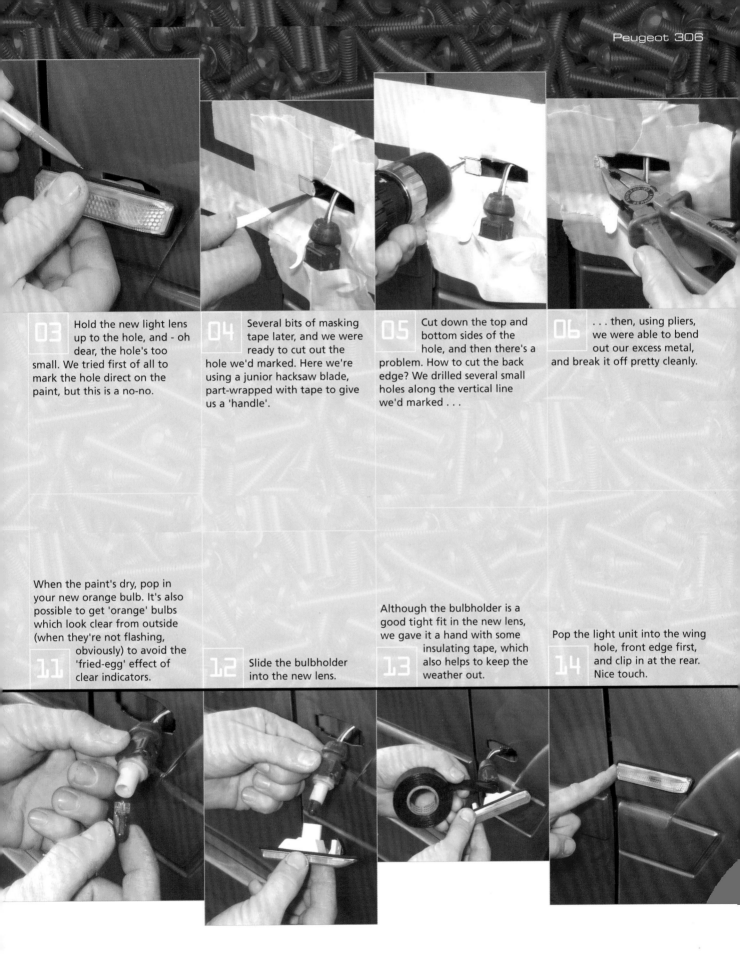

03 Hold the new light lens up to the hole, and - oh dear, the hole's too small. We tried first of all to mark the hole direct on the paint, but this is a no-no.

04 Several bits of masking tape later, and we were ready to cut out the hole we'd marked. Here we're using a junior hacksaw blade, part-wrapped with tape to give us a 'handle'.

05 Cut down the top and bottom sides of the hole, and then there's a problem. How to cut the back edge? We drilled several small holes along the vertical line we'd marked . . .

06 . . . then, using pliers, we were able to bend out our excess metal, and break it off pretty cleanly.

When the paint's dry, pop in your new orange bulb. It's also possible to get 'orange' bulbs which look clear from outside (when they're not flashing, obviously) to avoid the 'fried-egg' effect of clear indicators.

11

12 Slide the bulbholder into the new lens.

Although the bulbholder is a good tight fit in the new lens, we gave it a hand with some insulating tape, which also helps to keep the weather out.

13

Pop the light unit into the wing hole, front edge first, and clip in at the rear. Nice touch.

14

Wheels & tyres

Your most important decision?

Alloy wheels are the most important styling decision you'll ever make. No matter how good the rest of your car is, choose some cheap rims and your car will never look right. Choose a good set and you're already well on the way to creating a sorted motor. Take your time and pick wisely - wheel fashions change like the weather, and you don't want to spend shedloads on a set of uncool alloys.

Alloys and insurance

Before we go any further into which wheels are right for you, a word about insurance and security. Fitting tasty alloys to your 306 is one of the first and best ways to make it look cool. It follows, therefore, that someone of low moral standing might very well want to unbolt them from your car while you're not around.

Since fitting a set of alloys is one of the easiest bolt-on ways to mod a car, it's no surprise that the market in stolen alloys is as alive and kicking as it currently is. It's also not unknown for a set of wheels to go missing just for the tyres - if you've just splashed out on a set of fat Yokohamas, your wheels look even more tempting.

Tell your insurance company what you're fitting. They'll ask for the details, but are unlikely to charge you extra. You'll have to accept that they won't cover the extra cost of the wheels if they get nicked (or if the whole car goes). If you want the rims covered, it's best to talk to a company specialising in modified cars, or you could be asked to pay out the wheel cost again in premiums. The worst thing you can do is say nothing, and hope they don't find out - we don't want to go on about this, but there are plenty of documented cases where insurance companies have refused to pay out altogether, purely on the basis of undeclared alloy wheels.

Cheap alloys?

Hopefully, you'll be deciding which wheels to go for based on how they look, not how much they cost, but inevitably (for most ordinary people at least), price does become a factor. Some of the smaller manufacturers recognise this, and offer cheaper copies of more expensive designs - this is fine as far as you're concerned, but what's the catch? Surely buying a cheaper wheel must have its pitfalls? Well, possibly - and some of them may not be so obvious.

Inevitably, cheaper wheels equal lower quality and may be made from lesser-grade alloys, and may not be subjected to the same exacting tests as those from the top manufacturers. The worst case scenario is that you could end up with a wheel which is slightly "porous".

The main disadvantage of porosity in an alloy wheel is that the air will leak slowly out, and over a matter of time the tyre will deflate. We're not saying the tyre will deflate overnight, but porosity could result in a loss of for example say 5 psi a week. If you check your tyre pressures every week, this will be no more than a bit of an inconvenience. A tyre running 5 psi down will affect the handling of the car and also result in the tyre scrubbing out quickly. If you don't check the pressures for two weeks, then the tyre is 10 psi down, and now we're talking dodgy handing and nasty tyre wear

Porous wheels also have difficulty in retaining their paint or lacquer finish, with flaking a known problem. If the lacquer or paint comes off, the alloy is then exposed to the elements. Keeping your alloys clean can be a chore at the best of times, but once the lacquer or paint starts to deteriorate, the brake dust and dirt will become ingrained in the surface of the alloy. Serious effort every time you clean, and the problem will only get worse - the more you scrub, the more the lacquer comes off. Add to this the joys of the British winter (salt + exposed alloy = corrosion) and your wheels will start to look very second-hand, very quickly.

Buying wheels from established, popular manufacturers with a large range has another hidden benefit, too. It stands to reason that choosing a popular wheel will mean that more suppliers will stock it, and the manufacturers themselves will make plenty of them. Okay, so what? Well, if you're unlucky enough to have an accident which results in non-repairable damage to one wheel, you're going to need a replacement. If you've chosen the rarest wheels on the planet, you could be faced with having to replace a complete set of four, to get them all matching... A popular wheel, even if it's a few years old, might be easier to source.

Keep them clean

It's a small point maybe, but you'll obviously want your wheels to look as smart as possible, as often as possible - so how easy are they going to be to clean? The multi-spokers are hell to clean - a toothbrush job - do you really want this much aggro every week? The simpler the design, the easier time you'll have. There are plenty of good products out there to make your life less of a cleaning nightmare, but stay away from the very strong cleaners which can do more harm than good.

Locking bolts

Don't forget about locking wheel bolts (see "Hold on to your wheels" further on) - bargain these into a wheel/tyre package if you're buying new.

A word of warning about re-using your existing wheel bolts, should you be upgrading from steel wheels. Most steel-wheel bolts are not suitable for use with alloy wheels (and vice-versa). Make sure you ask about this when buying new wheels, and if necessary, bargain a set of bolts into the price.

Tricks 'n' tips
If you're keeping a steel wheel as your spare (or even if you're keeping an original alloy), keep a set of your original wheel bolts in a bag inside the spare wheel. Locking bolts especially might be too long when fitted to a thin steel wheel, and might jam up your brakes!

Tricks 'n' tips
It's worth applying a bit of car polish to the wheels - provided it's good stuff, and you can be sure of getting the residue out of the corners and edges, a polished wheel will always be easier to clean off than an unpolished one.

Other options

If you're on a really tight budget, and perhaps own a base model 306, don't overlook the possibility of fitting a set of standard alloys discarded by a GTI-6 owner - check that the bolt pattern's the same, obviously.

Size matters

The trend in wheel size is an interesting one. It seems that, for us Brits, biggest is best - there are 306s out there with 18s and up. But in general it's safe to say that you can't be seen with anything less than 17-inchers. In Europe, meanwhile, they're mad for the small-wheel look, still with seriously dropped suspension of course, but on 14- and 15-inch rims. On many cars (the 306 included), 16-inch rims are the biggest you can sensibly fit before you might have to start looking at sorting the arches, and they will improve the handling.

To be honest, successfully fitting big wheels in combination with lowered suspension is one of the major challenges to the modifier. With the 306, at least there's a bit more space under the arches than on some potential Max motors. As much as anything, it's tyre width that ultimately leads to problems, not so much the increased wheel diameter.

If the tyres are simply too wide, they will first of all rub on the suspension strut (ie on the inside edge of the tyre). Also, the inside edges may rub on the arches on full steering lock - check left and right. Rubbing on the inside edges can be cured by fitting spacers or offsets between the wheel and hub, which effectively move the wheel outwards, "spacing" it away from its normal position (this also has the effect of widening the car's track, which may improve the on-limit handling - or not). Fitting spacers must be done using special longer wheel bolts, as the standard ones may only engage into the hubs by a few threads, which is highly dangerous (also check that your locking bolts are long enough).

Rubbing on the outside edges is a simple case of wheelarch lip fouling, which must be cured by rolling out and cutting off the wheelarch return edge, and other mods. If you've gone for really wide tyres, the outer edge of the tyre will probably be visible outside the wheelarch, and this is a no-no (it's illegal, and you must cover it up). The only solution there is to fit a wide-arch kit.

The other trick with fitting immense alloys is of course to avoid the "4x4 off-roader" look, which you will achieve remarkably easily just by bolting on a set of 17s with standard suspension. The massive increase in ground clearance is fine for a bit of off-roading, but won't win much admiration at a cruise. Overcoming this problem can be a matter almost of inspired guesswork, as much as anything - especially if the budget won't stretch to a set of coilovers (see "Suspension").

Jargon explained

PCD – Is your Pitch Circle Diameter, which relates to the spacing of your wheel bolt holes, or "stud pattern". It is expressed by the diameter of a notional circle which passes through the centre of your wheel bolts, and the number of bolts. If, for instance, the PCD is 100 mm with four bolts, it's given as 100/4.

ROLLING RADIUS – is the distance from the wheel centre to the outer edge of the tyre, or effectively, half the overall diameter.

OFFSET - this is determined by the distance from the wheel mounting face in relation to its centre-line. The offset figure is denoted by ET (no, I mustn't), which stands for einpress tiefe in German, or pressed-in depth (now I know you're asleep). The lower the offset, the more the wheels will stick out. Fitting wheels with the wrong offset might bring the wheel into too-close contact with the brake and suspension bits, or with the arches. Very specialised area - seek advice from the wheel manufacturers if you're going for a very radical size (or even if you're not).

Speedo error?

One side-effect of fitting massive wheels is that your car appears to go slower. As the wheel diameter increases, so does its circumference (distance around the outside) - this means that, to travel say one mile, a large wheel will turn less than a smaller wheel. Because the speedometer is driven from the gearbox final drive, the apparent vehicle speed is actually based on the number of complete revolutions of the wheel. Therefore, for a given actual speed, a car with larger wheels will produce a lower speedo reading than one with smaller wheels - but it's not actually going any slower. This is not a great problem, just remember to compensate accordingly when driving in 30 and 40 zones.

The effects of increased wheel size are masked slightly by the fact that, as wheel size goes up, tyre profile (sidewall height) comes down, so one or two inches on wheel diameter might not mean any increase in overall wheel and tyre diameter.

that is dangerous on safety grounds should the locking bolts not be up to the required standard.

Obviously, you must carry the special key or tool which came with your bolts with you at all times, in case of a puncture, or if you're having any other work done, such as new brakes or tyres. The best thing to do is rig this onto your keyring, so that it's with you, but not left in the car. Don't leave it in the glovebox or the boot...that's the first place they'll look.

Hold on to your wheels

The trouble with fitting big wheels is that they are bolted on, and are just as easily bolted off, if you don't make life difficult for the thieves. If you have to park outside at night (ie. no garage), you could wake up one morning to a car that's literally been slammed on the deck! Add to this the fact that your car isn't going anywhere without wheels, plus the damage which will be done to exhaust, fuel and brake pipes from dropping on its belly, and it's suddenly a lot worse than losing a grand's worth of wheels and tyres.

The market and demand for stolen alloys is huge, and most people don't bother having them security-marked in any way, so once a set of wheels disappears, they're almost impossible to trace. Security marking won't prevent the wheels from being stolen but it does have a deterrent effect It.

When choosing that car alarm, try and get one with an "anti-jacking" feature, because the thieves hate it. Imagine a metal saucer, with a metal ball sitting on a small magnet in the centre. If the saucer tilts in any direction, the ball rolls off the magnet, and sets off the alarm. Highly sensitive, and death to anyone trying to lift your car up for the purpose of removing the wheels. Simply having an alarm with anti-shock is probably not good enough, because a careful villain will probably be able to work so as not to create a strong enough vibration to trigger it.

Cheap locking wheel bolts will be effective as a deterrent to the inexpert thief (kids, in other words), but will probably only slow down the pro. If you fit a cheap set of locking bolts, they will use a hammer and thin chisel to crack off the locking bolt heads. Some bolts can easily be defeated by hammering a socket onto the bolt head, and undoing the locking bolt as normal, while some of the key-operated bolts are so pathetic that they can be beaten using a small screwdriver. So it's vital to choose the best bolts you can.

There seems to be some debate as to whether it's okay to fit more than one set of locking bolts to a car - some people value their wheels so highly that they've fitted three or four sets of bolts. The feeling against doing this is that the replacement locking bolts may not be made to the same standard as factory originals, and while it's okay to fit one set on security grounds, fitting more than

Tricks 'n' tips

A word of warning about re-using your existing wheel bolts, should you be upgrading from steel wheels. Most steel-wheel bolts are not suitable for use with alloy wheels (and vice-versa). Make sure you ask about this when buying new wheels, and if necessary, bargain a set of bolts into the price.

Another point to watch for is that the new wheel bolts are the correct length for your fitment, taking into account whether you've fitted spacers or not. Bolts that are too short are obviously dangerous, and ones that are too long can foul on drum brakes, and generally get in the way of any turning activities. If in doubt ask the retailer for advice. Always check that the wheels turn freely once they've been put on, and investigate any strange noises before you go off for a pose.

Changing a set of wheels

You might think you know all about this, but do you really? Okay, so you know you need a jack and wheelbrace (or socket and ratchet), but where are the jacking points? If you want to take more than one wheel off at a time, have you got any axle stands, and where do they go? If you've only ever had wheels and tyres fitted by a garage, chances are you're actually a beginner at this. It's surprising just how much damage you can do to your car, and to yourself, if you don't know what you're doing.

What to use

If you don't already have one, invest in a decent hydraulic (trolley) jack and a set of axle stands. The standard Peugeot jack supplied with the vehicle just isn't stable enough to rely on for anything else other than an emergency wheel change.

Lifting and lowering the car is so much easier with a trolley jack, and once the axle stands are in position, there's no way the car can come down on you. Never rely purely on the jack for support - remember that even a brand-new trolley jack could creep down if you haven't tightened the release valve fully, or possibly collapse under load. Never be tempted to use bricks, wooden blocks or anything else which you have to pile up, to support the car. A 306 isn't a small car, and if you want to find out just how solidly it's built, try crawling under it when it's resting on a few bricks.

When using a hydraulic jack or axle stand, it's good practice to place a block of wood between the jack/stand head and car. This helps to spread the load over a wider area, avoiding damage to the underside of the car, and also protecting the underbody coating. Cut a slot in the top of the block of wood; this slot can then be engaged with the lower lip of the sill when positioning the jack/stand under the sill jacking points.

Front jacking point on sill. Our bodykit has indents to indicate the jacking points, but don't jack under plastic!

Where to use it

If possible, always jack the car up on a solid, level surface (ideally, a concrete or Tarmac driveway). Jacking up on a rough or gravelled surface is not recommended, as the car's weight won't be evenly distributed, and the jack may slip. If you have to jack up the vehicle on a surface which isn't level, be sure to firmly chock at least one of the other wheels so that the car doesn't roll away as it is lifted. It's good practice to chock a wheel, even if the ground is 100% level.

Jacking up the front

Before jacking up the front of the car, pull the handbrake on firmly (you can also chock the rear wheels, if you don't trust your handbrake).

If you're taking the wheels off, loosen the wheel bolts before you start jacking up the car. It's easily forgotten, but you'll look pretty silly trying to undo the wheel bolts with the front wheels spinning in mid-air. Standard alloys might have an anti-theft cover fitted over the bolts, or one locking bolt - you'll need the special key (probably in the glovebox).

We'll assume you've got a trolley jack. The next question is - where to stick it? If you put the jack under the sill, you can't add an axle stand later. An alternative front jacking point is the rear mounting points of the front suspension lower arms - jack up under there (with a nice flat offcut of wood on your jack head), and pop an axle stand (also with block of wood if poss) under the sill jacking point, marked by two little notches in the sill edge, or by an arrowhead marking. With the stand in place, you can lower the jack so the car's weight rests on the stand. We prefer to spread the weight between the stands and the jack, so don't lower the jack completely, unless you're jacking up the other side too.

Don't jack up the car, or stick stands under the car, anywhere other than kosher jacking and support points. This means - not the floorpan or the sump (you'll cave it in), and not under the brake/fuel pipes.

Jacking up the rear

When jacking up the rear of the car, place wooden chocks in front of the front wheels to stop it rolling forwards, and engage first gear.

If you're taking the wheels off, you don't have to loosen the wheel bolts before lifting the car, but you'll be relying on your handbrake to hold the wheels while you wrestle with the bolts. Better to loosen the rear wheel bolts on the ground.

To raise both rear wheels off the ground at the same time, you'll have to remove the spare wheel from its cradle to gain access to the rear crossmember. The rear of the car can then safely be lifted using a hydraulic jack positioned under the centre point of the rear crossmember (not the axle). With the vehicle raised, position an axle stand and block of wood beneath the rear jacking point on each sill. Set both stands to the required height, then slowly lower the jack whilst aligning the stand block slots with the lower lip of each sill. Ensure both stands are correctly positioned before removing the jack completely.

Remember not to put your axle stands under any pipes, or the fuel tank, and you should live to see another Christmas.

Finally...

As far as possible, don't leave the car unattended once it has been lifted. If it falls and hurts someone it would almost certainly be your fault.

Rear jacking point on sill. Don't jack under the plastic, or under the nearby fuel tank.

At a pinch, you can jack up under the rear damper lower mounting.

Tricks 'n' tips

Whenever you have your wheels off, clean off any hub corrosion with wet-and-dry paper, then coat the hub mating surfaces with copper (brake) grease - this "sticks" better than ordinary grease, and is temperature-resistant. There's no way you'll suffer stuck-on wheels again. "Proper" alloys come with a plastic collar which fits inside the wheel - this is an essential item which should not be discarded, as it centres the wheel properly and reduces wheel-to-hub corrosion.

Changing wheels

Before fitting your new wheels, there's stuff to check - first, have you got a plastic ring inside the hub (spigot)? Without it the wheel won't centre properly. It could cause damage to the the bolts.

Pop the wheel on, turning it to align the bolt holes, then in with the nicely-greased bolts, and tighten up as far as possible by hand. On the fronts (unless you've left it in gear) you won't be able to fully tighten the bolts anyway, as the wheels will spin. Keep your locking wheel bolt tool somewhere safe, but not obvious.

Always tighten the wheel bolts securely (ideally, to the correct torque - Peugeot's figure is 85 Nm, but check with your wheel manufacturer). This can only be done properly with the wheel back on the ground. Don't over-tighten the bolts, or you'll never get them undone at the roadside, should you have a flat. If your wheels have a centre cap of some kind, make sure you fit it. Not only does it look better, but in certain cases, the Allen key needed to undo it might be all the theft-deterrent you need, to stop an opportunist...

01 Equip yourself with some copper brake grease, and smear some on the wheel boss, inside.

02 You'll be doing yourself a favour if some of the same copper grease also finds its way onto the wheel bolt threads. Make sure the bolts are long enough to bite into the hub sufficiently.

03

04

Tyres

Tyres are the only thing keeping your car in contact with the road, so it figures that they're one of the most important components of your car. Saving a tenner (or more) a tyre might feel good when you pay the bill, but will you still feel the same way, the first time you blast down your favourite stretch of road, only to find yourself heading for a hedge mid-corner?

Choosing a known brand of tyre will prove to be one of your better decisions. Tyres are the only thing keeping you on the road, as in steering, braking and helping you round corners - what's the point of trying to improve the handling by fitting a quality suspension kit if you're going to throw the gains away by fitting naff tyres? Why beef up the brakes if the tyres won't bite? The combination of stiff suspension and cheap tyres is inherently dangerous - because the front end dives less with reduced suspension travel, the front tyres are far more likely to lock and skid under heavy braking. A problem with really wide tyres is aquaplaning - hit a big puddle at speed, and the tyre skates over the water without gripping - this is seriously scary when it first happens. Fitting good tyres won't prevent it, but it might increase your chances of staying in control. When choosing tyres listen to friends and fellow modifiers - real-world experience counts for a lot when choosing tyres (how well do they grip, wet or dry? How many miles can you get out of them?) Just make sure, before you spend your money on decent tyres, that you've cured all your rubbing and scrubbing issues, as nothing will rip your new tyres out faster.

Tricks 'n' tips

If you're buying a new set of wheels, most centres will offer you options on various set of tyres which they'll fit for you. Not only is this convenient, but it's usually top value too.

Marks on your sidewalls

Tyre sizes are expressed in a strange mixture of metric and imperial specs - we'll take a typical tyre size as an example:

205/40 R 17 V

for a 7-inch wide 17-inch rim

205 width of tyre in millimetres

40 this is the "aspect ratio" (or "profile") of the tyre, or the sidewall height in relation to tyre width, expressed as a percentage, in this case 40%. So - 40% of 205 mm = 82 mm, or the height of the tyre sidewall from the edge of the locating bead to the top of the tread.

R Radial.

17 Wheel diameter in inches.

V Speed rating (in this case, suitable for use up to 150 mph).

Not only is it essential to ensure the tyre is the right size for the rim, but the speed rating must also be suitable for the car. Tyres with an insufficient speed rating mean an MOT failure. This isn't a major problem on a base-model 306, but if you've got an XSi or GTI ensure all tyres fitted have at least a V rating (not that you'd consider fitting anything less anyway).

Pressure situation

Don't forget, when you're having your new tyres fitted, to ask what the recommended pressures should be, front and rear - it's unlikely that the Peugeot specs for this will be relevant to your new low-low profiles, but it's somewhere to start from. If the grease-monkey fitting your tyres is no help on this point, contact the tyre manufacturer - the big ones might even have a half-useful website. Running the tyres at the wrong pressures is a bad idea (you'll stand to wear them out much faster) and can be very dangerous (too soft - tyre rolls off the rim, too hard - tyre slides, no grip).

Speed ratings

Besides the tyre size, tyres are marked with a maximum speed rating, expressed as a letter code:

T up to 190 km/h (118 mph)

U up to 200 km/h (124 mph)

H up to 210 km/h (130 mph)

V inside tyre size markings (225/50 VR 16) over 210 km/h (130 mph)

V outside tyre size markings (185/55 R 15 V) up to 240 km/h (150 mph)

Z inside tyre size markings (255/40 ZR 17) over 240 km/h (150 mph)

If you've got marks on your sidewalls like this, you're in trouble - this has almost certainly been caused by "kerbing".

Lower your 306

If your Pug's still sitting on standard suspension, but you've decided you couldn't wait to fit your big alloys, the chances are it is now doing a passable impression of a tractor. Lowered suspension is an essential fitment, then - so how low do you go, and what side-effects will a lowering kit have?

One reason for lowering is, of course, to make your car look cool. Standard suspension nearly always seems to be set too soft and too high - a nicely lowered motor stands out instantly. Lowering your car should also improve the handling. Dropping the car on its suspension brings the car's centre of gravity closer to its roll and pitch centres, which helps to pin it to the road in corners and under braking - combined with stiffer springs and shocks, this reduces body roll and increases the tyre contact patch on the road. But - if improving the handling is really important to you, choose your new suspension carefully. If you go the cheap route, or want extreme lowering, then making the car handle better might not be what you achieve…

How low to go?

Assuming you want to slam your suspension so that your arches just clear the tops of your rims, there's another small problem - it takes some inspired guesswork (or hours of careful measuring and head-scratching) to assess the required drop accurately, and avoid that nasty rubbing sound. Lowering springs and suspension kits will only produce a fixed amount of drop - this can range from 20 mm to a more extreme drop of anything up to 80 mm. Take as many measurements as possible, and ask around your mates - although suppliers and manufacturers may be your best source of help in special cases. Coilovers have a range of adjustment possible, which is far more satisfactory - at a price.

Torsion bars

The 306's torsion bar rear suspension doesn't use coil springs, but instead uses hefty steel bars. The steel bars are splined at each end, and link each trailing arm to the opposite end of the axle crossmember; one is positioned in front of the crossmember and the other behind it. These steel bars twist as the suspension moves

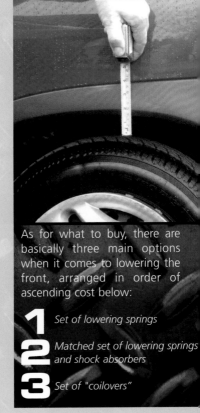

As for what to buy, there are basically three main options when it comes to lowering the front, arranged in order of ascending cost below:

1 *Set of lowering springs*

2 *Matched set of lowering springs and shock absorbers*

3 *Set of "coilovers"*

up and down throughout its travel, and it's the bars' resistance to this twisting (or torsional force) which provides the rear suspension springing. Another steel bar passes through the centre of the rear axle crossmember and links both trailing arms - this is the anti-roll bar, which is stiffer than the other two, but otherwise functions on the same principle.

Resetting the rear ride height is an involved procedure - not especially difficult or dangerous, but fiddly (and you could be playing for a long time before giving up and taking it to a garage). On an older car, you could also be facing the possibility of rusted-in bits, and a slide-hammer is the only answer if you get into that. The positive side though, is that you can lower the rear ride height without purchasing any new springs - the only cost involved is the labour.

Lowering springs - cheap and cheerful

The cheapest option by far, for lowering the front end. Lowering springs are, effectively, shorter versions of the standard items fitted to your 306 at the factory. With just a set of lowering springs, you fit new springs and keep the original shock absorbers (or dampers). Even if the original dampers are in good nick, just fitting uprated springs is a bit of a compromise. The original dampers work in harmony with the original springs - by uprating the springs without changing the dampers, you end up with a situation where the dampers and springs are mis-matched.

Fitting lowering springs will have the desired effect on the appearance of the car, but the mis-matched springs and dampers could adversely effect the handling. A very hard and choppy ride is another problem with taking the cheap option. If you drive your car hard, bear this in mind. You'd be much better off going for a full suspension kit with matched dampers and springs, which will ensure predicable handling. If the cost prohibits this and lowering springs are the only option for now, at least buy branded items of decent quality.

Fitting lowering springs

Quite an involved procedure this, and you'll need the correct tools for the job. A set of coil spring compressors is essential equipment

- no way can you remove the struts safely without them. A balljoint separator will probably be needed to disconnect the steering track rod balljoints. If you haven't got a set of spring compressors and can't beg/steal/borrow some, you ought to leave this one to the professionals.

If you've got the tools, the procedure is almost identical to fitting a full kit, the difference being that you are not fitting new damper cartridges in the strut, so follow the procedure but ignore the bits to do with the damper unit.

Coilovers

If you've chosen coilovers - you obviously know quality when you see it, and you're not prepared to compromise. True, quality costs, but you get what you pay for. This is the most expensive option, but it offers one vital feature - true adjustability of ride height (at the front). This means that you can make the finest of tweaks to lower your car over your rims. This also gives you more scope to fit those big rims now, lower it down as far as poss, then wait 'til next month before you have the arches rolled, and drop it down to the deck. Coilovers are a variation on the suspension kit theme, in that they are a set of matched springs and dampers, but with the added bonus of being fully adjustable (within certain limits obviously).

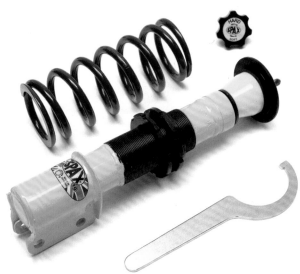

Front suspension

So - you want to get your 306's front end nearer the tarmac? You should be able to achieve this with a spring kit and the right equipment. You will need to either hire or buy some spring compressors, plus you'll need a set of Torx bits for your ratchet, then all the usual stuff like spanners, WD-40 and your biggest mate.

01 Spax's suspension kit comes with lowering springs and uprated dampers which essentially are the struts on which the springs mount

02 The standard MacPherson strut arrangement is easy to work on once the car is sitting on axle stands and the front wheel has been removed.

> **Attention!**
> *Proper spring compressors are essential to do this job safely. Don't try to manage without. When using the compressors, make sure they are securely fitted. Handle the compressed spring gently - it contains a lot of stored-up energy.*

07 Rotate the strut back and forth and it should free up enough to pull it free of the lower mounting. You may need to push the disc/caliper down slightly to give you some more room (this is where your big mate comes in).

08 Remove the strut completely, unscrew the compressors gently to release the spring, then take the spring top cup, spring, strut cover and rubber bump stop off.

09 You can now start assembling all the parts on to the new strut, exactly as they went on the old strut.

10 We found with the Spax kit that the bumpstop needed cutting in half, in order to give the car more suspension travel.

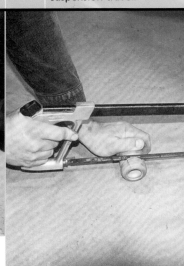

03 This is the anti-roll bar connection point, which is slightly tricky in that it has a Torx-ended thread and a locking nut. You have to keep the thread fixed as you undo the nut. It's a poor design and our Torx fitting failed on one side, which meant we couldn't re-tighten the nut when the job was finished and had to buy a new anti-roll bar push-rod.

04 Undo the bolt which tightens the hub spindle around the bottom of the strut.

05 Flip the protective cap off the strut top thread. Next, undo the locking nut, keeping the thread fixed by using an Allen key in the end.

06 You will need to use spring compressors to reduce the spring's height in order to remove from the arch. Go easy here and make sure you mount the compressors at opposite sides of the spring so it squeezes the spring evenly.

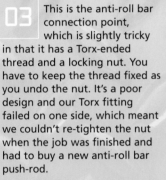

Place the concertina plastic cover in place noting that the bottom of it sits over the brass collar. The plastic cover must be fitted to protect the strut's centre **11** shaft from any muck and debris thrown up by the wheels.

The strut should be fully assembled before it's put back inside the arch. Note that the spring sits in one position only. You will almost certainly need to use the spring compressors again, although they won't need **12** to be compressed fully because of the new spring's reduced height.

The new Spax equipment fitted inside the arch. It will stop the Peugeot wallowing in bends, improve cornering speed and provide the driver with a much **13** better feel for what's going on beneath them.

The drop in height is obvious as soon as the car is back on its wheels – it looks sweet with the big rims back on. Once the car is driven the spring will **14** compress slightly further as it settles down.

Rear
suspension

Word of warning – the 306 isn't like some other hatches at the rear end. Instead of springs to support the ride it uses torsion bars, one for each side. These run transversely between the back wheels, about six inches apart and with a huge tube between them which houses the anti-roll bar. The bars themselves are, like most suspension torsion bars, splined to allow height adjustment.

But, and here's the trick, Peugeot have put a different number of splines on each end of the bars, thus allowing almost infinite height adjustment. This is okay if you have a workshop and the correct equipment to work with, but if like us you're working with regular tools plus one or two hired items, we would strongly recommend you don't attempt this work as you could come very unstuck. We had a nightmare getting the ride height the same on each side, taking apart the driver's side suspension around 20 times before getting it right. By then several objects had left the garage, and not all by the door, which wasn't open anyway.

So, while we've pictured the vital steps here, it doesn't show anywhere near what's involved in this complex process. Therefore, your best bet is to trust this work to a company or individual who has done the job before. It could save you a lot of time off-the-road.

Fortunately, at least one area of the suspension isn't tricky, that being the dampers. With one bolt top and bottom, a damper can be removed in less than 1/2-hour, so within two hours you can at least have uprated units fitted to your 306.

Torsion bar

Remove the bolt which connects the anti-roll bar arm to the suspension arm and holds the brake pipe/handbrake cable in place.

01

05 Back off the screw in the end of the torsion bar. It will only undo so far, as it's captive.

This is the anti-roll bar arm, which is duplicated on the other side. You have to release the bolts on both sides before this arm will rotate

02 downwards and out of the way of the torsion bar end.

Remove the pipe from

03 this bracket to prevent it being stretched.

You need to tackle both sides of the rear suspension at once, hence undo this slim

04 nut and remove it on the nearside and offside.

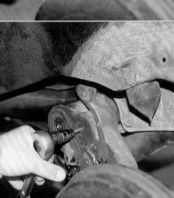

Using a Torx bit,

06 remove the screw in the end of the torsion bar.

The eccentric washer

07 has to be removed as it holds the torsion bar in place along with the captive screw at the other end.

We used a bolt with

08 our slide hammer to fix it inside the torsion bar, which has a threaded hole in its centre.

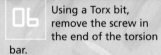

09 Before attempting to pull out the torsion bar, we marked its position relative to the suspension arm with a scriber.

10 Even on a car with as little mileage as ours (20K), the torsion bars can prove a headache to remove. We tore the thread out of two slide hammer ends before welding the end on, which did the job.

11 Here you can see the splines we're talking about. The splines this end disengage a fraction before the ones at the other end do, thus allowing you to make adjustments on either end. Unfortunately, this bar had come out too far so we'd disengaged both ends. We put the bar back in as it came out, then tried again. Just two outer splines dropped the ride by about 30mm (approx 15mm per spline). Reverse these steps to put the rear suspension back together.

Dampers

01 The Spax rear dampers are simple yet very effective. Best of all, they're fitted in a few hours.

02 Hidden away up inside the arch is the nut for the bolt going through the top of the damper . . .

03 . . . the best way to get at it is with a flexible joint and long extension bar. You will probably need a spanner on the other side too, to stop it spinning.

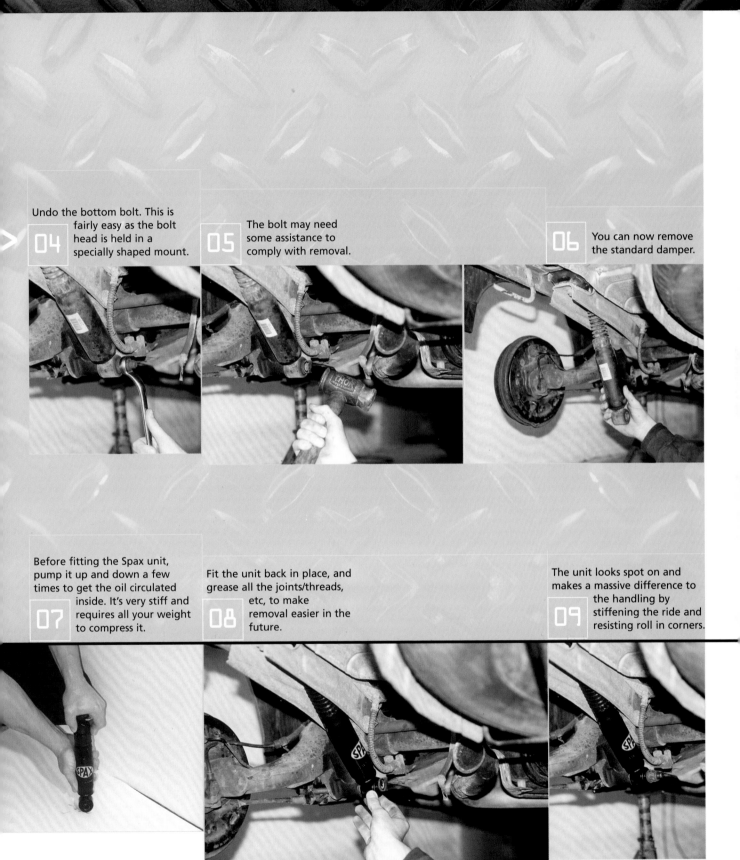

04 Undo the bottom bolt. This is fairly easy as the bolt head is held in a specially shaped mount.

05 The bolt may need some assistance to comply with removal.

06 You can now remove the standard damper.

07 Before fitting the Spax unit, pump it up and down a few times to get the oil circulated inside. It's very stiff and requires all your weight to compress it.

08 Fit the unit back in place, and grease all the joints/threads, etc, to make removal easier in the future.

09 The unit looks spot on and makes a massive difference to the handling by stiffening the ride and resisting roll in corners.

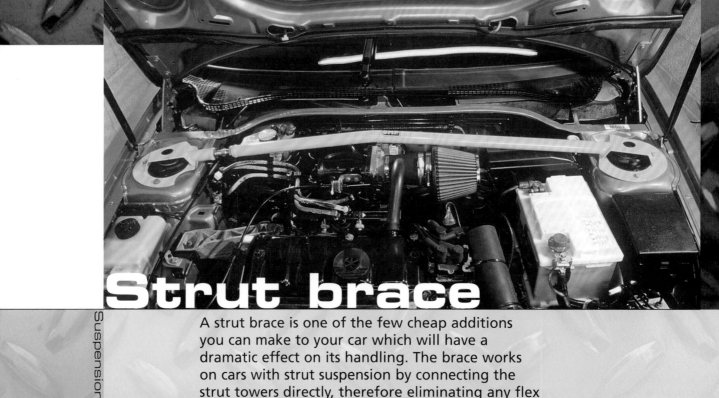

Strut brace

A strut brace is one of the few cheap additions you can make to your car which will have a dramatic effect on its handling. The brace works on cars with strut suspension by connecting the strut towers directly, therefore eliminating any flex within them. The effect this has is to make your car's bodyshell stiffer at the front end, which in turn makes the suspension react better. plus it keeps the strut geometry stable through hard cornering. You'll notice your car will be more predictable on the limit, plus more responsive at any speed. One from the likes of Momo, as we've chosen, is good in that it has a built-in adjuster to cope with variations in factory standards.

03 Refit the passenger side bolts and tighten to 20 Nm with a torque wrench.

04 Note that the driver's side bolt holes will probably be misaligned, so the brace needs adjusting.

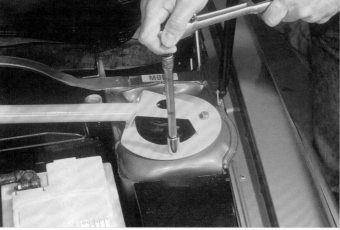

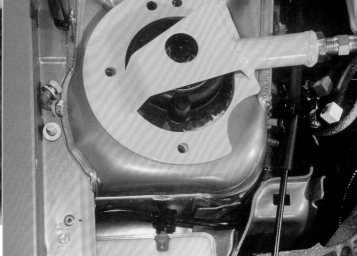

01 Start by undoing the bolts in each strut tower. Do this with the car's weight on the ground (ie don't jack the car up at all), then the bolt holes won't move.

02 Position the brace with the Momo sticker so it can be read from the front of the car.

Adjust the centre nuts so the holes line up on the driver's side strut top, then retighten the brace's lock nuts.

Refit the driver's side bolts and torque them up, then take the car for a drive and see what a difference the brace makes to handling and the car's rigidity.

05 Slacken the lock nuts either side of the adjusting nut.

06

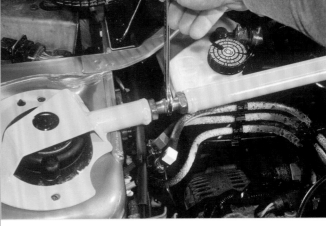

The middle pedal

It's not as if the standard 306 brakes aren't up to the job, but those of you without the all-disc XSi/GTI setup might still yearn for beefier brakes. Being able to stop quickly is always a bonus, we find, especially if your 306 is now a rocket-ship.

Uprating the brakes is actually a very easy bolt-on upgrade, but it'll be a complete waste of time if you're a cheapskate on tyres. Cheap, no-name tyres or remoulds won't be able to translate extra braking power into actual vehicle-stopping power - they'll give up their grip on the tarmac and skid everywhere.

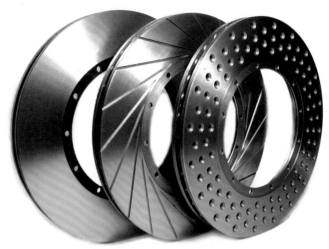

Grooved or drilled?

Besides the various brands of performance brake pads that go with them, the main brake upgrade is to fit performance front discs. Discs are available in three main types – grooved, cross-drilled and combinations of both.

Grooved discs (which can be had with varying numbers of grooves) serve a dual purpose - the grooves provide a "channel" to help the heat escape, and they also help to de-glaze the pad surface, cleaning up the pads every time they're used. Some of the discs are made from higher-friction metal than normal discs, too, and a good set can greatly improve braking performance.

Cross-drilled discs offer another route to heat dissipation, but one which can present some problems. In extreme cases cross-drilled discs can crack around the drilled holes, after serious use. The trouble is that the heat "migrates" to the drilled holes (as was intended), but the heat build-up can be extreme, and the constant heating/cooling cycle can stress the metal to the point where it will crack. Discs which have been damaged in this way are extremely dangerous. Only fit discs of this type from established manufacturers and check them regularly.

Performance discs also have a reputation for warping (nasty vibrations felt through the pedal). Now this may be so, but of course, the harder you use your brakes, the greater the heat you'll generate. Cheap discs, or ones which have had a hard time over umpteen thousands of miles, probably will warp. So buy quality, and don't get too heroic on the brakes for too long a period of time.

Performance pads can be fitted to any brake discs, including the standard ones, but are designed to work best with heat-dissipating discs. Don't be tempted to go much further than "fast road" pads - anything more competition-orientated may take too long to come up to temperature on the road, and might leave you with less braking than before.

Lastly, fitting all the performance brake bits in the world is no use if your calipers have seized up. If, when you strip out your old pads, you find that one pad's worn more than the other, or that both pads have worn more on the left wheel than the right, your caliper pistons are sticking. Sometimes you can free them off by pushing them back into the caliper, but this could be a garage job to fix. If you drive around with sticking calipers, you'll eat pads and discs. Your choice.

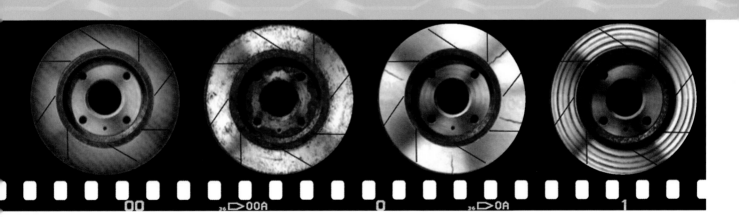

Front discs and pads

All 2-litre 306s come with four-wheel discs, as do models with ABS, but other models come with front discs and drums at the rear. If you ignore the fact drums don't look great behind big rims, they at least work well enough in the stopping department, even with fast road use. The fronts however could always do with a bit of help in making more effective use of your foot pressure on the pedal, which means increasing the friction between pads and discs. Also, grooves in the disc help both disperse the pad material as it wears and to cool the discs.

Red Dot's Fast Road Pads and vented/grooved discs are a direct replacement for the standard set-up and so are relatively simple to install. Not only will these perform better, they'll improve the appearance of your rims by highlighting modifications you've made behind them. Here's how to do the job, which will take no more than a few hours.

One word of warning here is to make sure you properly bed-in the new pads and discs. This is done by using the brakes lightly for the first 200 miles or so, then once this running-in period is over, use the brakes progressively harder in several stops, until brake fade is felt, then go for a long drive to let the brakes cool down (they'll be extremely hot). Don't let the pads cool off with the car stationary because this could cause hot spots on the disc.

By following the bedding-in process you'll get the best possible contact area on your brakes before hard use, which means eyeball-popping stopping power.

01 The kit is made up of two replacement discs and a pair of improved compound pads for either side. Note the pads have a wear indicator wire, which is used on some 306 models but not our XSi.

02 First you must jack up the car, support it on an axle stand then remove the wheel.

03 Using a Torx bit, undo the two bolts which hold the disc in place.

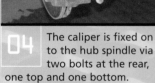

04 The caliper is fixed on to the hub spindle via two bolts at the rear, one top and one bottom.

05 Remove the caliper and ideally cable tie it up so it's not hanging by the brake hose, which could damage it.

06 You can now remove the disc, though as it locates tightly on the hub it may require a soft mallet to dislodge it.

07 Now remove the disc and, if it has plenty of metal remaining (over 18mm on vented ones, or 8mm on solid type), keep it - otherwise throw it away.

Attention!
If you disconnect the brake caliper hose, you'll have to bleed the brake hydraulic system afterwards, otherwise the brakes won't work. You'll also be mopping up spills of brake fluid, which is nasty stuff. See your Haynes manual for details.

Attention!
Brake dust from old pads may contain asbestos. Wear a mask to avoid inhaling it. Dispose of old braking system components safely at your local waste recycling centre - don't just put them in the bin.

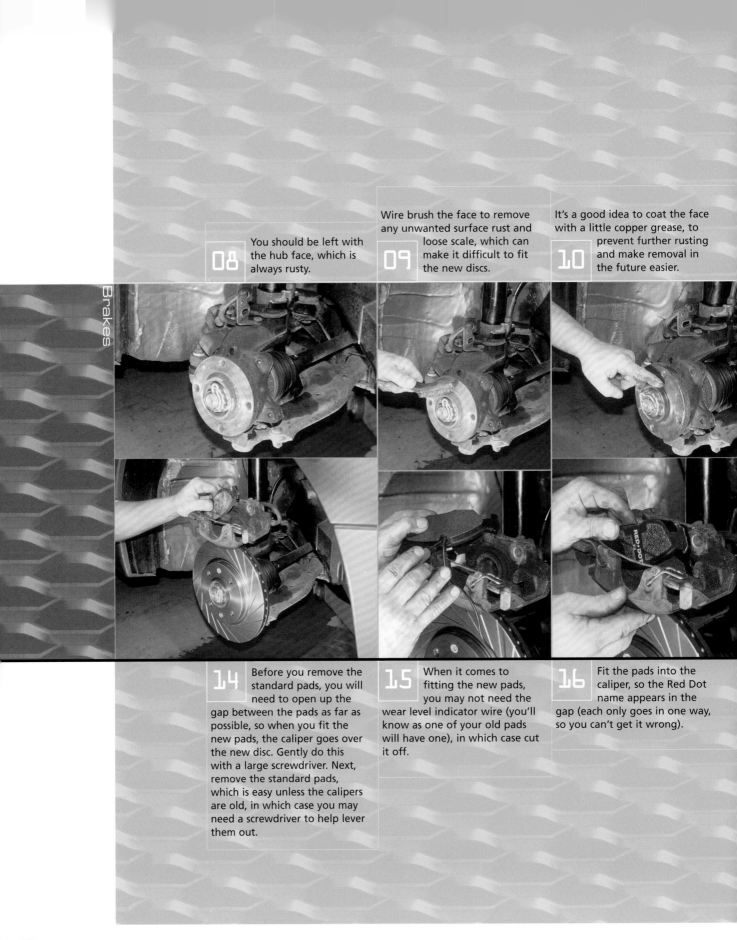

08 You should be left with the hub face, which is always rusty.

09 Wire brush the face to remove any unwanted surface rust and loose scale, which can make it difficult to fit the new discs.

10 It's a good idea to coat the face with a little copper grease, to prevent further rusting and make removal in the future easier.

14 Before you remove the standard pads, you will need to open up the gap between the pads as far as possible, so when you fit the new pads, the caliper goes over the new disc. Gently do this with a large screwdriver. Next, remove the standard pads, which is easy unless the calipers are old, in which case you may need a screwdriver to help lever them out.

15 When it comes to fitting the new pads, you may not need the wear level indicator wire (you'll know as one of your old pads will have one), in which case cut it off.

16 Fit the pads into the caliper, so the Red Dot name appears in the gap (each only goes in one way, so you can't get it wrong).

11 Fit the new discs and align the screw holes. Note that Red Dot discs with 20 or 40 grooves should have the grooves sloping down towards the rear of the car (as here), whereas 6 or 12 groove discs slope down towards the front.

12 Fit and tighten the screws.

13 Before the calipers and pads are put into place, the disc needs to be wiped over with a solvent to remove the grease and oil left after manufacture. Do this with a solvent such as meths.

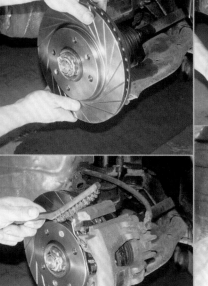

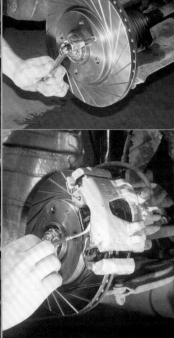

17 With the discs and pads looking so clean, you should dress up the caliper to suit, so first wire brush it to remove old brake dust and surface rust, being sure to get into all the crevices.

18 After cleaning with a solvent and cloth, paint the caliper whatever colour you wish. We chose silver Hammerite Smooth and used a child's paint brush and plenty of patience.

19 The finished job looks the business and by painting the caliper it'll be easier to clean when the wheels are done. Pump the brake pedal several times to reposition the pads. Then, bed in the discs and pads as per our intro, before you go steaming into a bend.

Painting
calipers

One downside to fitting big alloys is that it exposes your standard brakes. One option is to paint some of the brake parts so they look a nicer (red is common, but isn't the only choice). Only the 2.0 litre 306s (or those with ABS) have rear discs, but painting the brake drums is acceptable. Painting the calipers requires that they're really clean. Accessory stores sell aerosol brake cleaner for removing brake dust. Some kits come complete with cleaner spray.

01 We know you won't necessarily want to hear this, but the best way to paint the calipers is to do some dismantling first. The kits say you don't have to, but you'll get a much better result from a few minutes' extra work. Remove the calipers as described in the brake pad section. You don't have to detach the brake hoses, but make sure that you support the calipers so that the hose is not under pressure. Clean the calipers using brake cleaner, making sure that you remove all the dirt and muck.

Tricks 'n' tips
If you have trouble reassembling your brakes after painting, you probably got carried away and put on too much paint. We found that, once it was fully dry, the excess paint could be trimmed off with a knife.

02 Remove the caliper mounting bracket as described in the brake disc section. Again, clean it thoroughly using brake cleaner, followed by a wire brush.

03 Carefully paint the mounting bracket and caliper body. make sure you don't get paint on areas where pads, discs or piston touch. Don't paint the caliper piston. Allow to dry and apply a second coat if required. Refit your bits.

Attention!
If you disconnect the brake caliper hose, you'll have to bleed the brake hydraulic system afterwards, otherwise the brakes won't work. You'll also be mopping up spills of brake fluid, which is nasty stuff. See your Haynes manual for details.

*The finished
drum looks
much better
behind a big rim.
far better than a
black and rusty
blob, eh?*

Painting
rear
drums

What do you do with those ugly drums sat on the back of your car? Well, in an ideal world you swap in a set of discs and calipers from a higher performance model, but most of us can't afford that, though we can at least make the drums look half-decent.

When you have spare hour, get the rims off and paint the drums. You have a choice of colours with specialist caliper paint available from various suppliers, though Hammerite Smooth can do just as good a job, plus it holds well if you prepare the drums properly. Ideally you should remove the drums altogether and prepare/paint them on the ground, on some paper. However, you can just as easily mask up the arch and spray them, or simply paint the drums by brush.

Attention!
Brake dust from old pads may contain asbestos. Wear a mask to avoid inhaling it. Dispose of old braking system components safely at your local waste recycling centre - don't just put them in the bin.

A rotary wire brush does the business in getting rid of rust and flaking paint. You don't need to get the drums back to bare metal, but if yours are seriously rusty you may want to consider either new drums or a rust curing solution prior to painting.

01

We used Hammerite Smooth in silver. Even being brushed, it tends to smooth out so doesn't leave a 'brushed-on' finish. Spray painting would still provide a better quality finish, however.

02

Leave the drum to dry for about an hour and apply a second coat, then a third if it needs it though this is unlikely in a brush application.

03

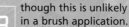

Interiors

With a dashboard of mostly black plastic, and only a few very subtle highlights in dark grey around the fascia, the 306 doesn't exactly look king of the hill. Sure, you may have given it a top head unit, but that's not going to be enough when it comes to people checking out your ride. And the standard plastic parts like steering wheel, gearknob and handbrake just aren't saying the right things and will no way do justice to your driving. The dash does at least have everything in the right place and within easy reach, however, and with a few choice additions has the potential to stand out in a crowd.

Take it easy and break less

If a piece of trim won't come off, don't force it. If something feels like it's going to break, it probably will - stop and consider whether to go on and break it, or try another approach. Especially on an older car, things either never come off as easily as you think, or else have already been off so many times that they either break or won't fit back on properly. While we'd all like to do a perfect job every time, working on an older car will, sooner or later, teach you the fine art of 'bodging' (finding valid alternative ways of fixing things!). Bodging is fine (if you've no choice) with interior and exterior trim, but make sure there are no safety implications - gluing an exterior mirror on might just about work with the car stood still, but it's going to fall off half a mile down the road, isn't it? Any Tricks 'n' Tips we give in our procedures are things we've tried ourselves, which we know will work. Also, don't assume that you'll have to bodge something back on, every time - if a trim clip breaks when you take something off, it might be easier and cheaper than you think to simply go to your Peugeot dealer, and buy a new clip.

The halfway-house to a fully-plated interior is to make up your own tailored mats. Start by trimming up a piece of card to fit the curvy bits . . .

01

. . . then mark round onto some hardboard. The makers say not to fit their 'plate over carpets, because it'll flex too much and crack. For those of you who didn't know, most chequer is actually plastic look-alike, and it won't stand having your size 9s hoofing on it for long, so make up a solid-ish backing.

02

With the hardboard marked up, it's out with the jigsaw for some trimming, then try it in place. You only need a board for the flat part of the floor (where your feet go) - the 'plate can go behind the pedals unsupported.

03

Much try-and-trim later, you'll be ready to attack the silvery stuff. Mark it up . . .

04

Fully-tailored
chequer mats

05 . . . and trim it to shape. One advantage of being plastic is that it's easy to cut!

06 When it comes to the tricky bits, lay it in and mark it roughly before cutting. Cut it too big to begin with, 'cos you can always trim more off.

07 Now take the 'plate out and mount it on the board. Use plenty of spray-on adhesive. You'll need something heavy-ish to press the two together while the glue dries - we chose one of our new rims, which did the job just fine.

08 Et voilà! The finished result. Okay, so you've spotted it's not a 306. But the effect's the same.

Tricks 'n' tips

What about using one of your existing floor mats as a template? It's somewhere to start, anyway.

01 The easy option is to buy mats with chequerplate inserts. Another option is to buy separate chequerplates to fit to existing carpets, or to other mats.

02 Lay the plate into position on your mat, then take some Tipp-Ex, and dab a spot through the four holes in the plate.

03 Using a sharp implement, poke a hole through the mat where the spots were.

04 Bring the plate back in, and fit the first anodised "washer" and bolt through . . .

Chequerplate
heel mats

05 . . . so that the bolt pokes through the mat, and the large round "nut" can be screwed on the back.

06 Tighten the bolt with an Allen key. Repeat this so that all four corners of the plate are pinned on.

07 Our kit came with a load of stick-on Velcro pads, which can be stuck to the underside of the round "nuts", and to the four corners of the mat itself.

08 And now - the finished result.

Ally door pins

Making little additions like these door pins can make all the difference in your ride. It shows you've paid attention to those extra few bits that make your interior that bit more performance enhanced than the next guy's. Actually installing them is more involved than you might think, but there's nothing overly complicated about the job, it's just time consuming so give yourself a couple of hours.

01 The kit consists of two pins (each with two grub screws) plus an Allen key.

02 Start the job by removing the removing the door panel, which first means prising out the door handle surround.

03 Prise out the electric window switches and remove the connector on the rear.

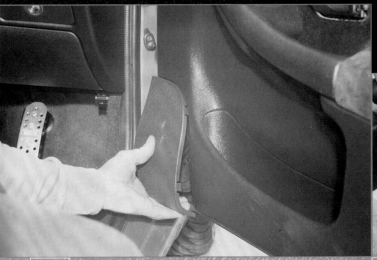

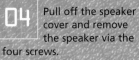

04 Pull off the speaker cover and remove the speaker via the four screws.

05 Ease out the screw cover plug up near the door frame.

06 Undo the first Torx screw of three, which holds on the upper section of the door panel.

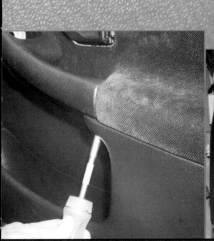

07 Undo the second screw which holds the centre of the door panel to the door.

08 The last screw is behind the electric window buttons.

09 Now pop off the door panel, taking care to lift it over the plastic door pin.

10 The door pin can now be seen.

11 The aluminium pin needs to be no higher than the standard one otherwise the upper grub screw won't have anything to tighten on.

12 The plastic pin is stuck in place and you could use a junior hacksaw to remove it, but for speed we found a Dremel handy tool was ideal.

13 Remove the split door pin and you'll note there's a small flat on the metal rod. The aluminium pin won't go over this so, using a small file, remove the flat area.

14 Push the pin into place and you should feel it bottom out.

15 Tighten the grub screws evenly top and bottom. Replace the door panel and you'll have a new, chunky door pin.

White dials

Peugeot's mostly black dashboard looks far too 'normal' for performance use. The items you can fit around the dash fascia can make a big difference, but the one area which you stare at most during driving is desperate for work. White dials will totally transform your dash and they're essential on a tuned car.

Early white gauge kits were always tricky to fit as they involved removing the needles in order to swap fascias. If you weren't careful you would end up with needles being reluctant to go back on, or worse still, breaking. The great thing about Lockwood's kit is that it doesn't require any needles to be removed and therefore is loads easier.

With the right tools, which means a set of Torx bits and a very sharp knife (ideally a scalpel) you can have your dials swapped for something more interesting in around half a day and it'll look like a professional's done the work.

>>

01 Lockwood's white dial kit comes in two parts, and has a set of four black stick-on washers which we'll get to later.

02 To get to the gauge housing you first have to remove the steering shroud, which is held on by three Torx screws from underneath.

03 Remove the shroud, which comes apart in an upper and lower half. The top needs to be taken out altogether.

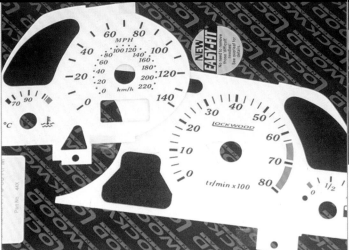

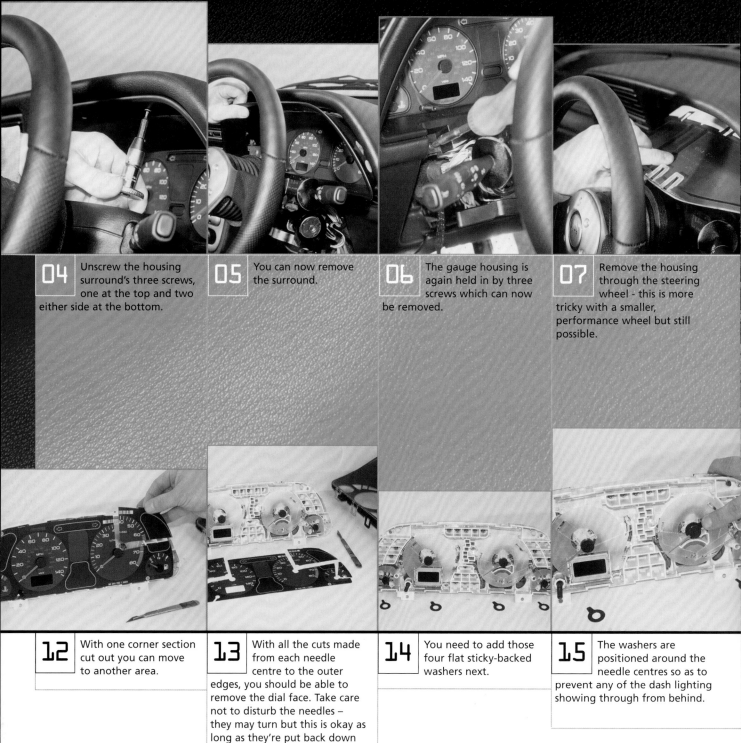

04 Unscrew the housing surround's three screws, one at the top and two either side at the bottom.

05 You can now remove the surround.

06 The gauge housing is again held in by three screws which can now be removed.

07 Remove the housing through the steering wheel - this is more tricky with a smaller, performance wheel but still possible.

12 With one corner section cut out you can move to another area.

13 With all the cuts made from each needle centre to the outer edges, you should be able to remove the dial face. Take care not to disturb the needles – they may turn but this is okay as long as they're put back down to zero once the new white dial face is in position.

14 You need to add those four flat sticky-backed washers next.

15 The washers are positioned around the needle centres so as to prevent any of the dash lighting showing through from behind.

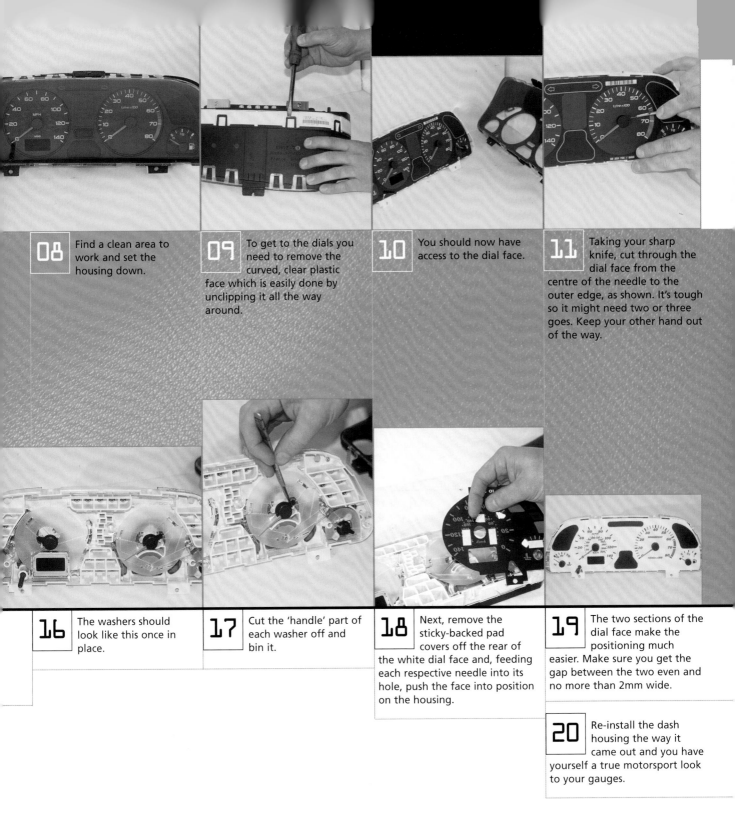

08 Find a clean area to work and set the housing down.

09 To get to the dials you need to remove the curved, clear plastic face which is easily done by unclipping it all the way around.

10 You should now have access to the dial face.

11 Taking your sharp knife, cut through the dial face from the centre of the needle to the outer edge, as shown. It's tough so it might need two or three goes. Keep your other hand out of the way.

16 The washers should look like this once in place.

17 Cut the 'handle' part of each washer off and bin it.

18 Next, remove the sticky-backed pad covers off the rear of the white dial face and, feeding each respective needle into its hole, push the face into position on the housing.

19 The two sections of the dial face make the positioning much easier. Make sure you get the gap between the two even and no more than 2mm wide.

20 Re-install the dash housing the way it came out and you have yourself a true motorsport look to your gauges.

Gearknob

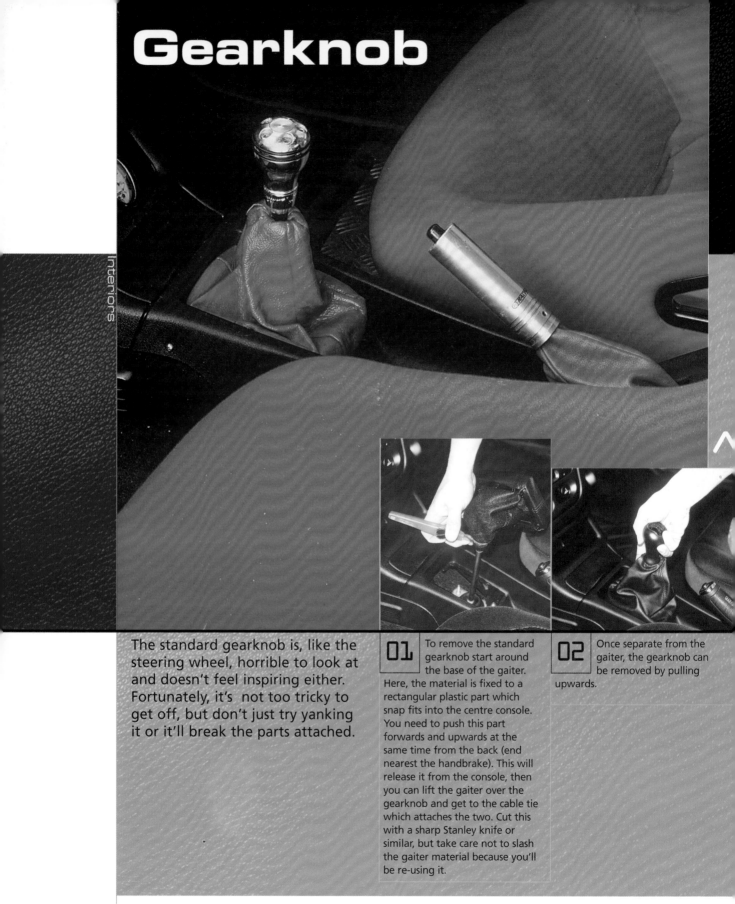

The standard gearknob is, like the steering wheel, horrible to look at and doesn't feel inspiring either. Fortunately, it's not too tricky to get off, but don't just try yanking it or it'll break the parts attached.

01 To remove the standard gearknob start around the base of the gaiter. Here, the material is fixed to a rectangular plastic part which snap fits into the centre console. You need to push this part forwards and upwards at the same time from the back (end nearest the handbrake). This will release it from the console, then you can lift the gaiter over the gearknob and get to the cable tie which attaches the two. Cut this with a sharp Stanley knife or similar, but take care not to slash the gaiter material because you'll be re-using it.

02 Once separate from the gaiter, the gearknob can be removed by pulling upwards.

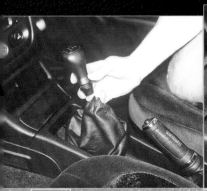

03 The gearknob is a tight fit so takes some brute force, but it will come off.

04 You should now be left with the zinc plated gearstick which has a white plastic surround at the top end. The plastic has to stay because it gives the Momo gearknob locating screws something to grip on.

05 Next, put the gaiter back over the gearstick but don't press it back in the console just yet. Put on the new Momo gearknob and unscrew the covering section at the bottom of the gearknob which reveals the three locating grub screws, then screw these into place in equal amounts.

06 Re-tighten the lower covering section of the gearknob, which should leave you with it all tight and feeling ready for a shift.

07 Turn the gaiter inside out and, with a new cable tie, tighten it around the narrowest part of the gaiter just under the gearknob's position.

08 When you now turn the gaiter back the right way and refit the base, it should look like the gaiter has never been removed. Line up the seams in the gaiter so it looks professional and you're all done.

Handbrake lever

The handbrake lever performs a simple function and on the average car gets used only while the car's stationary. But there are other times when it's needed (we'll say no more), so to make sure you get the best grip on it you need a good, fat handle.

Momo's handbrake conversion fits the bill perfectly and matches all the other parts we've used to dress up our 306's interior, so it's a must. You also need a gaiter to match the gearstick and that has to be fitted beforehand.

First you have the pleasure of removing the offending standard item. There's an easy and satisfying way to do this and it's with a Stanley knife. You need to cut the rubber handle which sits around the main metal part of the handbrake. With the handbrake on (ie up), start at the bottom (nearest the rear seat) and cut the underside of the rubber all the way up to the handbrake release button.

01

02

The rubber handle can be removed now, leaving you with the bare metal handbrake lever.

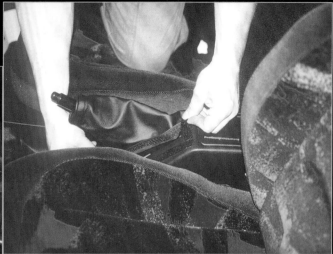

03 Fit the gaiter briefly to check where the Velcro strips (supplied) need to be applied. Wipe the area down with methylated spirits so the tape sticks, then cut the tape as necessary and apply

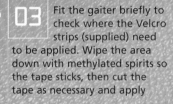

04 Slip the gaiter into place over the handbrake

05 Press down the gaiter edges against the Velcro. Check it all stays where it's supposed to with a few goes on the handbrake and it should be a permanent fixture.

The Momo handle is supplied with an adapter and screw cover. The screw cover locates in the gaiter and must go on before the handle, then the adapter sits over the end near the handbrake release button. With the handle in place, tighten the grub screws, making sure the release button sits proud of the handle by at least 5mm.

06

The section which covers the grub screws can then be pushed over the handle, so bringing the gaiter neatly into place.

07

Make sure the gaiter's isn't twisted but is free to move along with the handbrake lever. If all's okay, you're finished.

08

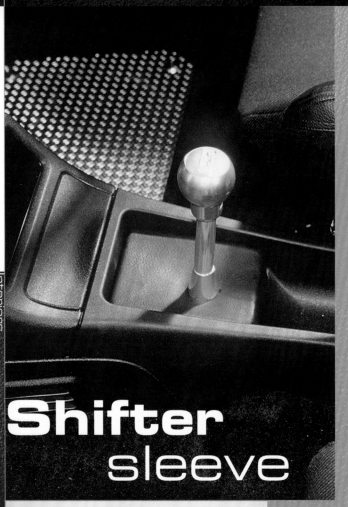

There are a number of parts available on the aftermarket to dress up your car's interior. Note we say 'cars' here and not 306, as many of the parts out there are universal and hence won't be specifically designed for a Peugeot. This gear shaft sleeve is such a part and requires your gearstick to be completely straight. Luckily, most front-wheel-drive cars do have such gearsticks so it can be used widely, though you have to do something with the 'baggy' gaiter in order to make the sleeve look worthwhile. In our case, we used the standard Peugeot gaiter material to cover the hole in the centre console, but it'd be a better idea to buy some new material from an interior specialist, so you have more to play with. Look to around three hours max to sort this out.

Shifter sleeve

04 Cut the seams of the material carefully with a sharp knife.

05 You should now have two halves of the gaiter, of which you'll use one (the other being a spare in case you screw up).

06 Fold the material around the gaiter housing to form a smooth look.

01 Remove the gear shaft gaiter from the centre console and find a clean area to work on it. Refer to the section on fitting the B & M short shifter for more info on getting the gaiter off.

02 Lever the clips from the gaiter housing to free the material.

04 Remove the gaiter from the housing and turn the material inside out.

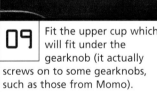
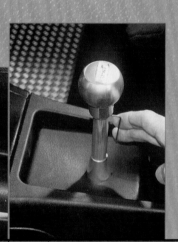

07 Refit the housing into the centre console, making a hole for the gear shaft.

08 Fit the Richbrook gear shaft sleeve lower half and tighten the grub screw.

09 Fit the upper cup which will fit under the gearknob (it actually screws on to some gearknobs, such as those from Momo).

10 Tighten the upper grub screw so the sleeve is secure against the shaft. Take care not to overtighten as the grub screw is very small. Replace the gearknob and you'll have the effect of a race-like aluminium gear stick.

Seats and harnesses

Comfort is a big part of enjoying your driving experience and the standard 306 provides plenty of it with its softly sprung suspension and well cushioned seats. In fact, the 306 offers better seating than in many other cars, but it still isn't good enough when the speed gets serious.

What you need is a seat that will grip as much of your body as possible, to prevent you sliding sideways and losing concentration while trying to discover the limit of your car's rubber. Yet you also need practicality if you still want to use the rear seats, which means recliners.

You might not shed any weight from the car by fitting new seats (only the fixed bucket seats tend to be significantly lighter), but you will gain a whole new driving experience out on the road and, if you want to do track days, you know you'll have the equipment necessary to hold you tightly in place as you get into four-wheel drifts.

Of all the seat manufacturers out there, Corbeau is one of the biggest names. Their products look and do the business, and one of the latest designs is the Carrera recliner. It offers excellent shoulder, hip and thigh support while providing space for a 4-point harness if so required. But using race harnesses is a headache if you drive your car regularly on the street, because once fixed in you can't lean forward to get the stereo or glove box or anything else on the dash.

The solution is to either keep the standard seat belt (naff) or to fit one of Safety Devices' 3-point retractable harnesses which gives you all the purposeful looks of a race harness but the movement of the standard belt. The Safety Devices belt does this by using a motion-activated switch, which senses any undue movement and locks the retractable section solid, much like a standard seat belt does when you try and yank it across your

01 body too quickly. First job is to remove the standard seats. The front, door-side fixing is easy to get to and is held in place by a Torx bolt like the others.

02 The centre console-side front bolt is one of the trickiest to get to, but with the seat full back and a long extension on a wrench it's just possible. Manoeuvring around the inside of the car to undo it is good practice for when the Corbeau seat goes back in.

>>

Next you can move the seat all the way forward and get to the rear bolts which, fortunately, are much **03** easier.

The door-side bolt should release the seat altogether. Make sure you keep the bolts somewhere safe as they **04** have to be re-used.

On models with an airbag, there is a belt tensioner on the driver's seat, connected to the wiring shown here. Disconnect the battery and wait for at least 10 minutes **05** before proceeding.

The belt tensioner is not used with our new set-up, so cut the wiring and wrap it with insulating tape before tucking it safely under the carpet. (This may make the airbag warning light stay on, in which case you'll have to remove the warning light bulb to **06** avoid an MOT failure.)

Attention!

1 The seat belt tensioner is an explosive device similar to the airbag (page 152) and must to treated with similar respect.

2 Later models may also have side airbags in the seat. We advise you not to remove this type of seat yourself.

3 If you remove either of these devices, you are disabling a safety-related system. Make sure you tell your insurance company.

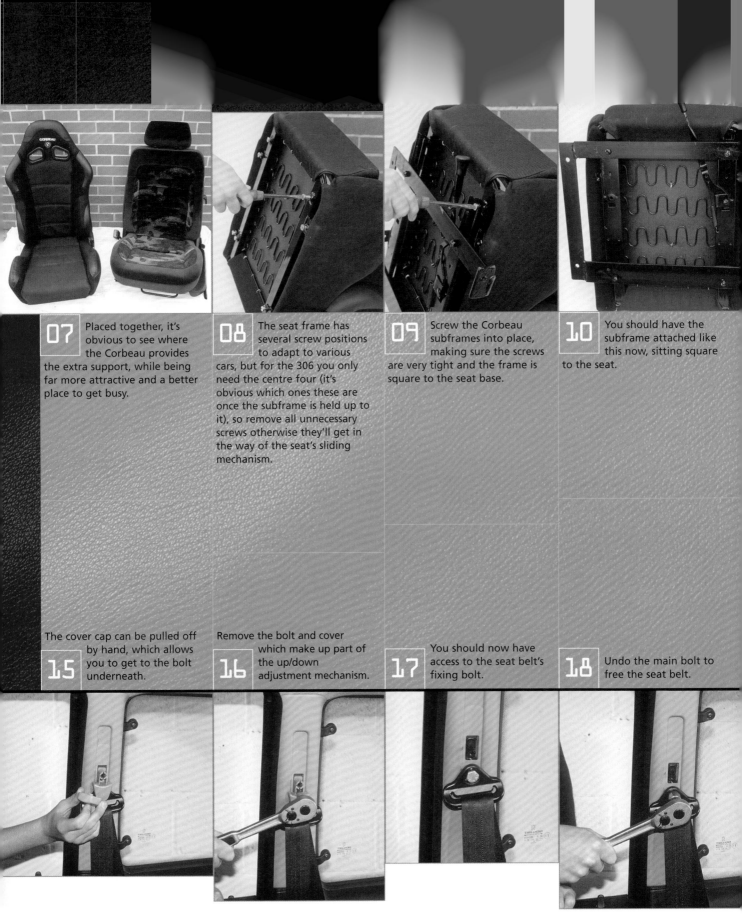

07 Placed together, it's obvious to see where the Corbeau provides the extra support, while being far more attractive and a better place to get busy.

08 The seat frame has several screw positions to adapt to various cars, but for the 306 you only need the centre four (it's obvious which ones these are once the subframe is held up to it), so remove all unnecessary screws otherwise they'll get in the way of the seat's sliding mechanism.

09 Screw the Corbeau subframes into place, making sure the screws are very tight and the frame is square to the seat base.

10 You should have the subframe attached like this now, sitting square to the seat.

15 The cover cap can be pulled off by hand, which allows you to get to the bolt underneath.

16 Remove the bolt and cover which make up part of the up/down adjustment mechanism.

17 You should now have access to the seat belt's fixing bolt.

18 Undo the main bolt to free the seat belt.

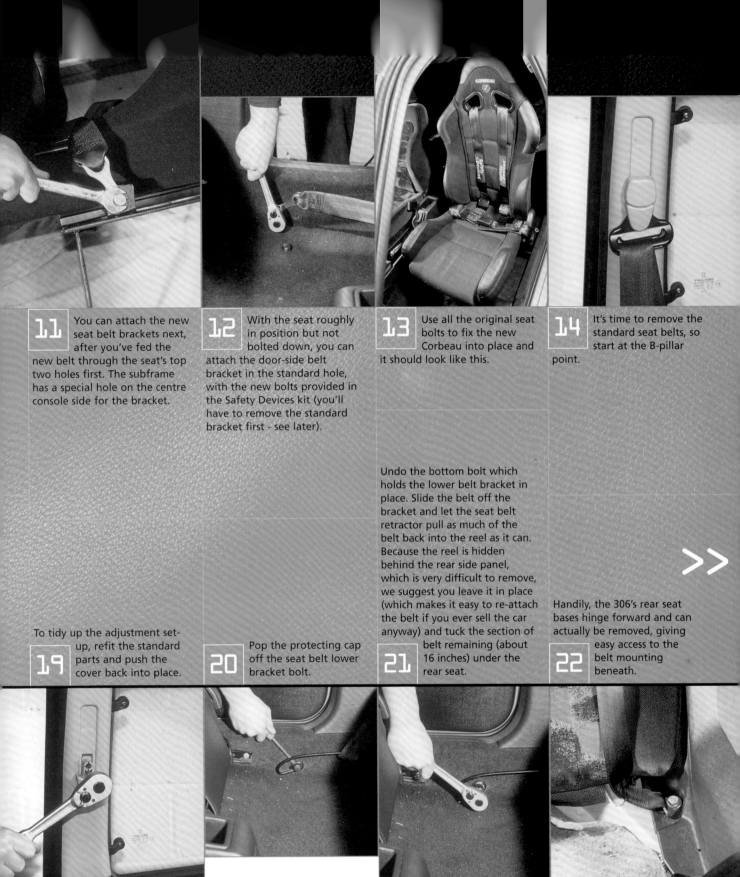

11 You can attach the new seat belt brackets next, after you've fed the new belt through the seat's top two holes first. The subframe has a special hole on the centre console side for the bracket.

12 With the seat roughly in position but not bolted down, you can attach the door-side belt bracket in the standard hole, with the new bolts provided in the Safety Devices kit (you'll have to remove the standard bracket first - see later).

13 Use all the original seat bolts to fix the new Corbeau into place and it should look like this.

14 It's time to remove the standard seat belts, so start at the B-pillar point.

Undo the bottom bolt which holds the lower belt bracket in place. Slide the belt off the bracket and let the seat belt retractor pull as much of the belt back into the reel as it can. Because the reel is hidden behind the rear side panel, which is very difficult to remove, we suggest you leave it in place (which makes it easy to re-attach the belt if you ever sell the car anyway) and tuck the section of belt remaining (about 16 inches) under the rear seat.

>>

Handily, the 306's rear seat bases hinge forward and can actually be removed, giving easy access to the belt mounting beneath.

19 To tidy up the adjustment set-up, refit the standard parts and push the cover back into place.

20 Pop the protecting cap off the seat belt lower bracket bolt.

21

22

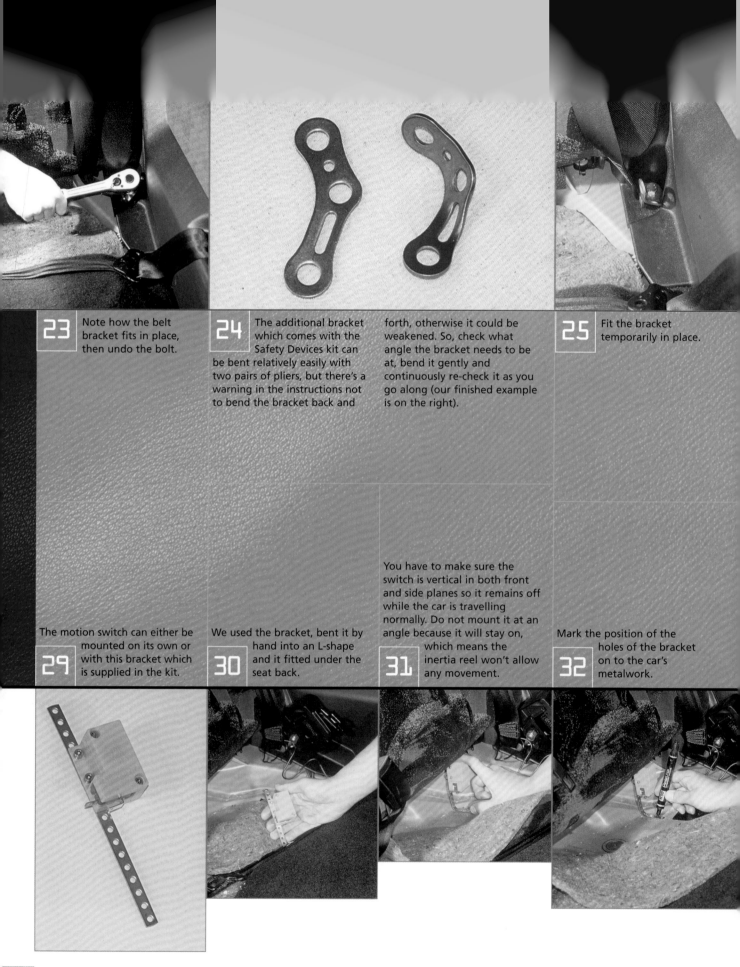

23 Note how the belt bracket fits in place, then undo the bolt.

24 The additional bracket which comes with the Safety Devices kit can be bent relatively easily with two pairs of pliers, but there's a warning in the instructions not to bend the bracket back and forth, otherwise it could be weakened. So, check what angle the bracket needs to be at, bend it gently and continuously re-check it as you go along (our finished example is on the right).

25 Fit the bracket temporarily in place.

29 The motion switch can either be mounted on its own or with this bracket which is supplied in the kit.

30 We used the bracket, bent it by hand into an L-shape and it fitted under the seat back.

31 You have to make sure the switch is vertical in both front and side planes so it remains off while the car is travelling normally. Do not mount it at an angle because it will stay on, which means the inertia reel won't allow any movement.

32 Mark the position of the holes of the bracket on to the car's metalwork.

146

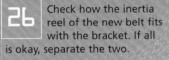

26 Check how the inertia reel of the new belt fits with the bracket. If all is okay, separate the two.

27 You can now put the motion switch's earth strap into place on the bolt.

28 You'll find it easiest to bolt the bracket in place first, then fit the inertia reel on to it, but you'll still find you need eight hands to do the job!

33 Remove the switch and drill 3mm holes where you've just marked.

34 Tighten the self-tapping screws in the holes to fix the unit into place.

35 The switch's position is out of the way, so even with the rear seat back in place it won't be affected.

36 With the other side's switch in place, you need to find a 12V source which is only on when the ignition is turned on. Luckily, the wiring harness which runs under the rear seat provided this, which we tested with a digital multimeter.

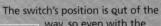
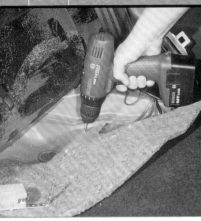

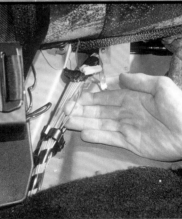

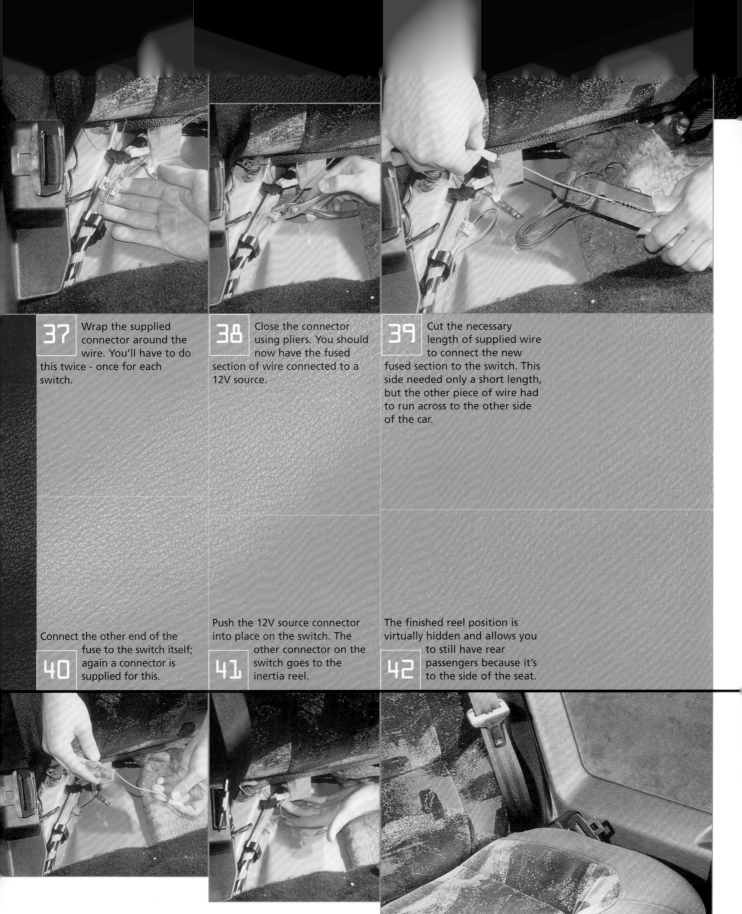

37 Wrap the supplied connector around the wire. You'll have to do this twice - once for each switch.

38 Close the connector using pliers. You should now have the fused section of wire connected to a 12V source.

39 Cut the necessary length of supplied wire to connect the new fused section to the switch. This side needed only a short length, but the other piece of wire had to run across to the other side of the car.

40 Connect the other end of the fuse to the switch itself; again a connector is supplied for this.

41 Push the 12V source connector into place on the switch. The other connector on the switch goes to the inertia reel.

42 The finished reel position is virtually hidden and allows you to still have rear passengers because it's to the side of the seat.

B & M short shifter

B&M are an American company who have been, in the past, known to produce only for their home market. Their quality is very good and the kits they produce are complete and easy to fit. It was only a matter of time before they saw sense in producing for the European and Japanese market.

The B&M Sport Shifter replaces the stock Peugeot gearstick, but uses all the standard housing parts. It reduces throw dramatically so makes your shifts quicker, plus it makes the gearbox easier and more performance biased to drive with.

01 The B&M kit comes complete with the stick itself (with anodised aluminium ball as opposed to the stock Peugeot's plastic piece), a fat ally gearknob, assembly grease, new bushes plus a new gaiter cable tie. Oh yeah, and the all-important window sticker.

02 Start the job by pulling the gearstick gaiter base out of the centre console, then up and over the gearknob. Cut the cable tie holding it on.

>>

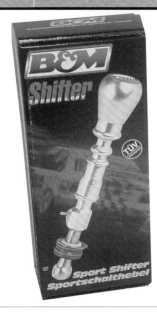

03 Remove the standard gearknob, it's well fixed so takes some pulling.

04 You should be able to pull the gearknob off separately from the gaiter, which can also be removed.

05 Below the gaiter, at the base of the gearstick, there are four nuts on the housing which need to be undone and removed.

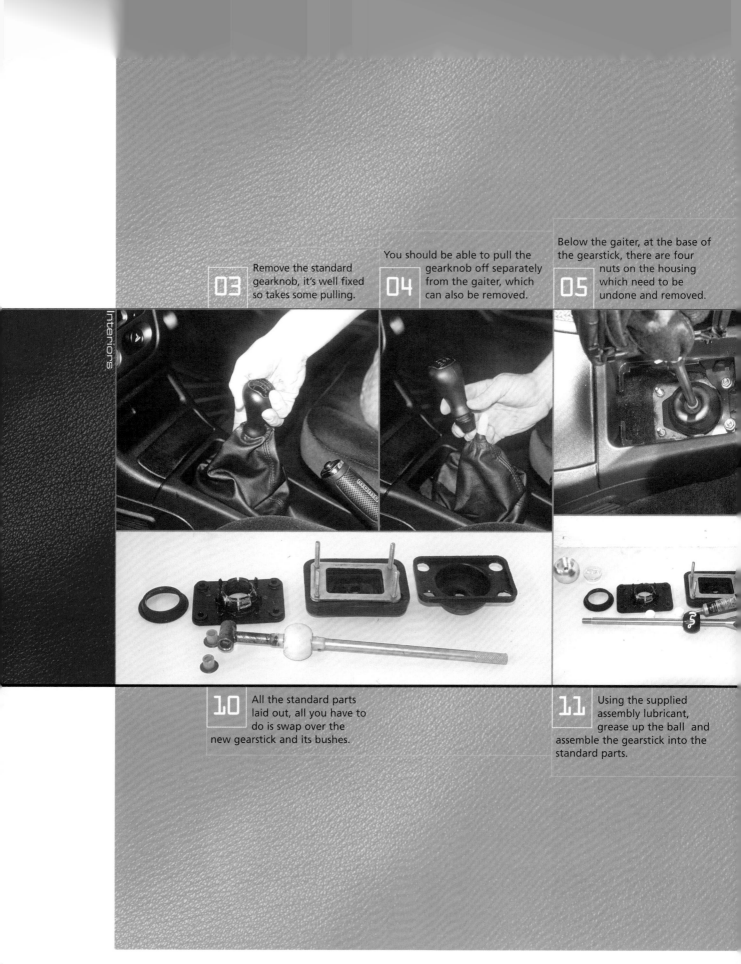

10 All the standard parts laid out, all you have to do is swap over the new gearstick and its bushes.

11 Using the supplied assembly lubricant, grease up the ball and assemble the gearstick into the standard parts.

06 Jack the car up, place it on axle stands and get underneath. Just above the exhaust you can see the gearstick linkage. Remove the bolt there which you can just about get to with open-ended spanners.

07 Push the gearstick down and out through the bottom of the car, then remove it from underneath. B&M say ideally you should remove the exhaust to do this, but we found it easy enough without all that hassle.

08 With the stock gearstick (right) next to the B&M, you can see the new one is shorter. What you can't see so well is the slightly increased distance between the ball and lower bolt hole, which is what reduces throw at the top of the gearstick.

09 Prise the fixing ring off the standard plastic socket.

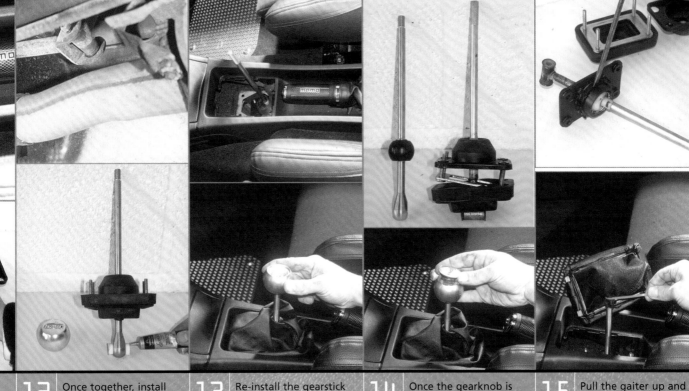

12 Once together, install the bushes and grease them too.

13 Re-install the gearstick and screw on the gearknob.

14 Once the gearknob is tight, you can install the top cap with the B&M logo on it, but make sure you wrap around the rubber band before it pushes into place.

15 Pull the gaiter up and over the gearstick and use the cable tie to tighten it up against the underside of the gearknob.

16 Ready for a drive?

Steering
wheel

The sooner you remove the great black blob of a standard wheel, the better. But there's one problem – the airbag. Before you start messing around undoing anything, disconnect the battery and wait for at least 10 minutes.

01 To remove the air bag and get at the main bolt holding the wheel on, use a Torx bit and undo the two bolts at the back.

02 Once the air bag bolts are undone (they stay retained within the back of the main wheel section), you can lift off the airbag and get to the orange electrical plug.

You'll need a larger Torx bit now to undo the main steering wheel bolt. This is usually tight so to provide resistance put the steering lock on by turning the wheel without the key in the ignition. Once the bolt is undone you should release the steering lock and line the wheel up so it's in the straight ahead position. You need to keep it positioned like this until you've fitted the new wheel.

Then there comes the job of getting the wheel off its splines – not easy. Even on a car with as little as 20K miles it can be tough to get the wheel off, so some gentle persuasion with a soft mallet might be needed. Be careful and hit the underside and main section of the wheel only, swinging from under the dash so if you do hit anything other than the wheel, it's not likely to show. Leave the wheel bolt screwed down a few turns so the wheel doesn't fly off when it comes free.

With the steering wheel removed it's time to get serious. The Momo wheel shown is typical of most aftermarket wheels in that it needs a separate boss on which to mount the wheel.

03 Disconnect the single orange two-pin plug which fits into the rear, then put the air bag somewhere it can't do any damage.

04 [positioned like this until you've fitted the new wheel.]

05 [turns so the wheel doesn't fly off when it comes free.]

06 [needs a separate boss on which to mount the wheel.]

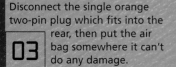

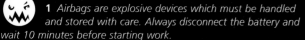

Attention!

1 Airbags are explosive devices which must be handled and stored with care. Always disconnect the battery and wait 10 minutes before starting work.
2 If you remove an airbag, you are disabling a safety-related system. Make sure you tell your insurance company.

07 The boss is the part which fits on to the splines on the end of the steering column. It has a notch cut of the underside and this has to slide into place one way over the plastic locator on the column. Then the boss has to be located on the splines with two opposing holes at 12 o'clock and 6 o'clock positions. There is also lettering on the boss saying 'TOP' which should sit to the left of the hole at 12 o'clock.

08 With the boss in position, replace the main steering wheel bolt but don't tighten it fully just yet.

09 On the Peugeot 306, as the horn button is on the left front stalk and not the steering wheel itself, you don't need the metal horn ring that the Momo kit is supplied with.

10 Next come the best bit – fitting the wheel itself. Just fit one Allen screw for the moment because you can use the wheel with or without the horn centre surround, for which you require two different Allen screws (both supplied in kit). With the surround the wheel has more of a luxury feel, without it has more of a motorsport look, so it's up to you. Either way, remember the horn push is not functional.

11 You need to fit the wire and fuse section which comes with the kit – the two pin connectors push into the orange plug to send a signal back to the car's ECU, thus preventing your air bag warning light coming on. Tuck the wires neatly out of the way inside the steering wheel boss.

12 Re-apply the steering lock and tighten the steering wheel main bolt.

13 We chose the more luxury look to go to with the silver theme inside our car and for this we need the longer, silver screws with come in the kit. There are, obviously, shorter black screws if you choose the motorsport look without the centre surround. Do the screws up with the Allen key provided.

14 Sit back and feel how different your driving experience will be, and notice how much more purposeful your 306 looks inside.

Pedals

Any part that is supplied as a universal fit is a part made with compromises. As such, it's going to fit no single car spot on. You should realise this with any aftermarket stuff you buy, though it's not always the part manufacturer's fault that their stuff doesn't fit.

01 On the 306 the foot pedals have huge steel arms on the rear, right in the centre. The problem is that the Sparco aluminium pedals are centre drilled and come with bolts just 10mm long. So, with a piece of metal 25mm deep and 5mm wide sitting right in the centre of the rear of each pedal, you can't drill where you want to.

02 We had to mount the aluminium pedal covers slightly off-centre, to the right. Mark the hole positions with a pen.

03 Drill the holes marked with a 3mm pilot hole first then to the full 10mm required for the bolts supplied.

04 Another problem was that the Sparco items are gently curved along their length, but it's a compromise curve to suit as many cars as possible. It didn't suit our accelerator and clutch, but it was easily solved by using a combination of large pliers and a flat-end screwdriver as a lever to bend the Peugeot's steel pedals to shape. Here the accelerator pedal is being bolted up.

05 Remove the pedal rubbers from the brake and clutch. Don't put them in the bin because you may need them again come MOT time.

06 Drill the other pedals and bolt the covers in place, then tighten all the bolts making sure that the locking nut for each bolt goes on far enough to thread into the nylon, otherwise the bolts and pedals could work loose and you don't want that as you're heel and toe'ing for a quick bend.

01 First clean and degrease- see the advice earlier in the section for painting.

On a heavily-grained finish, remember that the grain will show through thin film, and a deep grain means the film won't stick all over the surface. Not a good idea to go mad with the wet-and-dry (or Scotchbrite), to get rid of the grain - you'll destroy the surface totally.

02 Cut the film roughly to size, remembering to leave plenty of excess for trimming - it's also a good idea to have plenty to fold around the edges, because the film has a nasty habit of peeling off, otherwise.

03 Next, gently warm up both the panel, and the film itself.

04 Peel off the backing, being careful that the film stays as flat as possible. Also take care, when you pick the film up, that it doesn't stick to itself.

Applying film
panel

05 Stick the film on straight - very important with any patterned finish. Start at one edge or corner, and work across, to keep the air bubbles and creases to a minimum. If you get a really bad crease, it's best to unpeel a bit and try again - the adhesive's very tacky, and there's no movement available.

06 Work out the worst of the air bubbles with a soft cloth - get the stuff to stick as best you can before trimming, or it'll all go horribly wrong. To be sure it's stuck (especially important on a grained surface), go over it firmly with the edge of your least-important piece of "plastic" - not a credit card.

07 Once the film's basically laid on, it's time for trimming - which is the hard bit. We found it was much easier to trim up the tricky bits once the film had been warmed up using a hairdryer or heat gun, but don't overdo it. Make sure you've also got a very sharp knife - a blunt one will ripple the film, and may tear it.

08 To get the film to wrap neatly round a curved edge, make several slits almost up to the edge, then wrap each sliver of film around, and stick on firmly. If the film's heated as you do this, it wraps round and keeps its shape - meaning it shouldn't try and spring back, ruining all your hard work.

Window
tinting

The more uniform a car's appearance, ie the less clutter that's obvious from the outside, the smoother it'll look. That's why when you see tinted windows they can have a dramatic appearance – you can't see the seats inside, the seat belts, the parcel shelf and you can barely see through the car. But tinted windows are about more than just making your car look good (no, really), because they can reduce heat coming into the car. They also help keep the interior materials in the best condition by reflecting sunlight. And it's not just professionals who can make a good job, because with a little practice anyone can come up with good results.

01 The Folia Tec window tinting kit is universal and comes on a big roll. It'll do all side glass but for the rear window too it's possible you'll need two rolls. The kit comes with a squeegee, knife and bottle of solution which needs to be mixed with de-ionised (or distilled) water.

02 When doing a door, you need to remove the interior panel, so start with the electrics such as the window switches. It's wise to disconnect the battery too.

Attention!
There are legal limits to how dark you can make your windows. See "Legal Modding" on page 188 for details.

07 Remove the screw under the main handle.

08 Unclip the speaker cover and remove it.

09 Remove the speaker screws, disconnect the wires and take out the speaker completely.

10 Unclip the door panel all the way around and remove it.

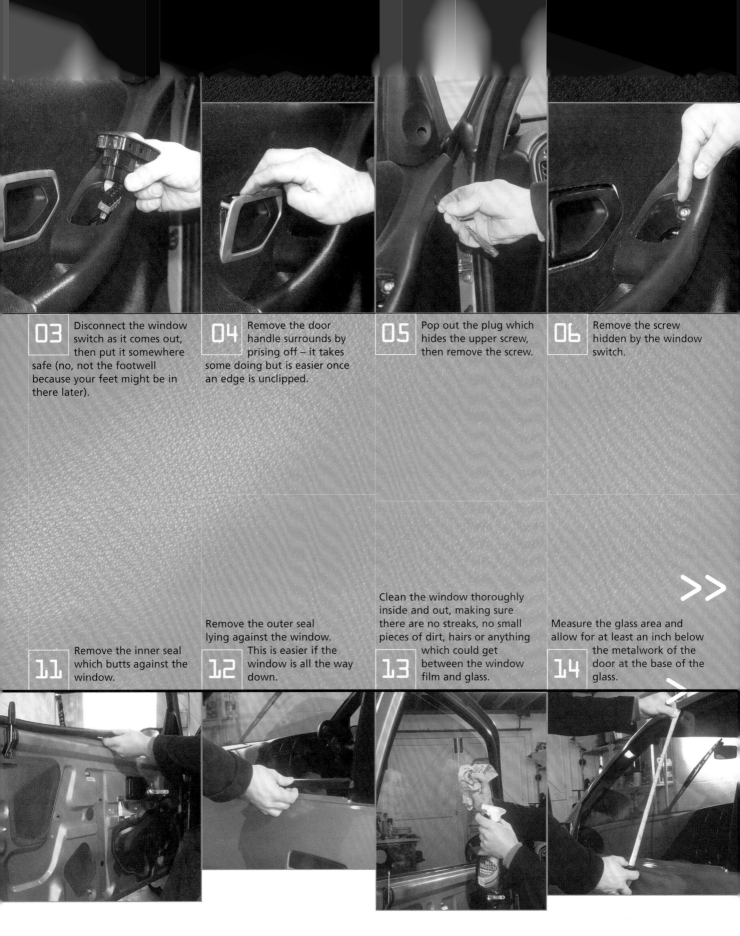

03 Disconnect the window switch as it comes out, then put it somewhere safe (no, not the footwell because your feet might be in there later).

04 Remove the door handle surrounds by prising off – it takes some doing but is easier once an edge is unclipped.

05 Pop out the plug which hides the upper screw, then remove the screw.

06 Remove the screw hidden by the window switch.

11 Remove the inner seal which butts against the window.

12 Remove the outer seal lying against the window. This is easier if the window is all the way down.

13 Clean the window thoroughly inside and out, making sure there are no streaks, no small pieces of dirt, hairs or anything which could get between the window film and glass.

>>

14 Measure the glass area and allow for at least an inch below the metalwork of the door at the base of the glass.

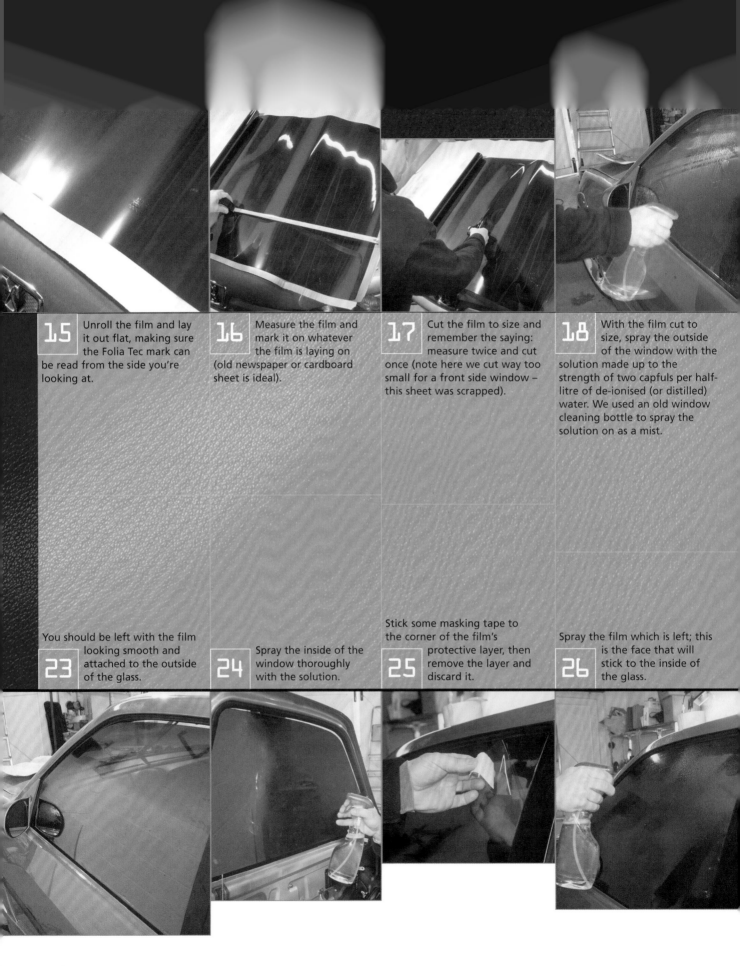

15 Unroll the film and lay it out flat, making sure the Folia Tec mark can be read from the side you're looking at.

16 Measure the film and mark it on whatever the film is laying on (old newspaper or cardboard sheet is ideal).

17 Cut the film to size and remember the saying: measure twice and cut once (note here we cut way too small for a front side window – this sheet was scrapped).

18 With the film cut to size, spray the outside of the window with the solution made up to the strength of two capfuls per half-litre of de-ionised (or distilled) water. We used an old window cleaning bottle to spray the solution on as a mist.

23 You should be left with the film looking smooth and attached to the outside of the glass.

24 Spray the inside of the window thoroughly with the solution.

25 Stick some masking tape to the corner of the film's protective layer, then remove the layer and discard it.

26 Spray the film which is left; this is the face that will stick to the inside of the glass.

19 Keeping the Folia Tec mark readable, stick the film to the outside of the glass.

20 Spray the film thoroughly with the solution once more.

21 Using the supplied squeegee, smooth the film against the glass right to the edges.

22 Using the supplied sharp knife, cut the film to size taking care not to tear it. At times we found it useful to hold the squeegee's straight edge against the side being cut.

27 Position the film inside of the glass, taking care not to crease it.

28 Using the squeegee, press the film on from the centre outwards, removing the air bubbles as you go.

29 There will probably be an excess of water which comes out, so have some tissue handy to soak it up at the edges.

The film takes some working to get all the bubbles and water out, but once done it should look the business from the outside.

ICE **Head** unit

The Alpine CD head unit we went for proved to be the easiest job in the whole installation, apart from screwing in the ready-made sub box. Once we'd fiddled with the Pug's head unit to get it out, the Alpine almost dropped in without being asked. Now that most cars and most sets come with ISO plugs and leads, getting a good head unit fitted is a not difficult. This lot took less than half an hour, even with taking photos.

01 Getting the original head unit out of the dash wasn't that difficult, and it didn't need any special tools either. At first glance there are no holes to stick removal keys into, but if you look closely at the lower edge of the unit, there are two slightly relieved areas where the keys would fit. Our chances of getting genuine Peugeot keys were minimal, so we improvised with feeler gauges instead. After sliding a couple of thick gauges into the slots, we felt the clips release and some jiggling got the unit to come out. It took about 30 seconds. Bargain.

02 Once we'd pulled the unit out, surprise, surprise, it really was a DIN-sized set after all. All we had to do then was disconnect it from the ISO wiring plugs, and remove its fitting cage which was clipped into the dash.

03 To make our new Alpine CD player look as well finished as the last unit, we got an Autoleads fascia trim that looked exactly like the surround of the head unit that came out. This new surround was fitted with the Alpine's cage, ready to accept the new unit.

04 Here's the Alpine all connected up to the original looms using its ISO-friendly connector. These ISO plugs are an industry standard now, so just about all cars and units come with them. If you get a set that doesn't have them, don't worry, you can buy ISO converters from Autoleads for almost every combination available. The RCA signal cable that's plugged into the head unit feeds a non-amplified audio signal to the amplifier mounted in the boot.

05 There we go, one head unit up and running. The only thing to be really careful about when you're doing your head unit swap is that you don't force the unit into the dash. If it doesn't want to go straight in something's caught up, so investigate and find out what's wrong instead of just shoving until something breaks, OK?

Amplifier and sub-woofer

A decent car stereo system is nothing without an amplifier, and even if your head unit reckons it's got 200 watts of power built in, it won't be a patch on the real deal. For the Peugeot's system we used a four-channel Sony amp to drive the front speakers and the sub woofer. The head unit could manage the rear speakers, which don't get that much use anyway.

Seeing as the Pug's MTX sub box is quite a size, we wanted to take up as little space as possible with the amp, so we went for a side-mounted rack that kept it out of the way. This left the maximum boot room left, and if the sub box is removed for carrying goodies, the amp won't be in the way.

Attention! MDF dust is nasty stuff to breathe in. Wear a mask when you're cutting, drilling or sanding it.

01 To get the Sony amplifier to fit in the Peugeot 306 we started off by making a cardboard template to the required shape. We used original Peugeot fixing points with much longer screws to hold the rack in position, and here we're looking for those screw holes using a thin probe. By using original fixings we didn't need to drill any new holes in the Pug, which is good when you come to remove the gear later.

02 Once we'd finalised the shape of the template, it was transferred to a piece of MDF and then drawn around. We also marked out the small holes for the mounting screws and the larger one where the Neutrik shelf connector was going to be fitted.

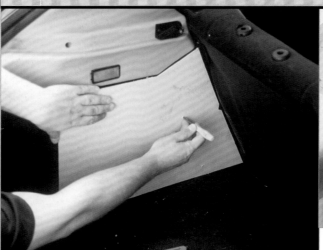

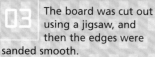

03 The board was cut out using a jigsaw, and then the edges were sanded smooth.

04 Next, we placed the amplifier on the rack and marked the mounting holes and wire holes, prior to drilling them out. This way the amp will be an easy fit when the rack is in place, and the wiring will neatly pop out from behind the board without trailing all over the boot.

05 After we trimmed the board with trunk-liner carpet, we screwed the amp into position and then fed the wiring through ready for attaching to the amplifier. As you can see, the wires have been terminated and then protected with heatshrink tubing. This also gives easily-visible colour-coding - red for positive, black for negative - to help with correct connections. The small connector in the top corner of the rack is the Neutrik quick-release connector used for the back shelf connections. It fits into the existing hole left by the Peugeot shelf connector, which can be re-installed when this system comes out.

06 This is the speaker cable that feeds the sub-woofer cabinet, and we've also given it the heatshrink treatment. The quick-fit terminals just need the wire to be stripped back and then clipped in place, making the box a simple fit.

07 One last thing to do is screw the box down to stop it sliding around the boot, and to keep it pinned in place if the car's involved in an accident. Always check on the other side of a panel before you drill through it to check nothing will be damaged when the drill pops through, OK?

08 The finished boot looks the part, and sounds better than a load of shopping from Tesco. There's still room for some stuff, and if you've got lots, what's wrong with the back seat? 'If you are going to carry anything sharp or heavy in the boot though, consider getting hold of an aftermarket grille to protect the sub cone from damage. Re-cone kits are expensive!

^

01 We fitted the JBL tweeters to the 306's A-pillar trims, which had to be removed before we could screw the tweeter in place. After pulling the door rubber down, the trim just unclipped from the pillar.

Front speakers

02 With the trim on the bench, the tweeter position was marked up. The tape on the trim showed the top level of the dashboard, so we knew not to fit the speaker lower than that.

03 After we'd marked where to make the holes, they were drilled out and then the mounting cup was screwed in place with the short screws supplied in the kit.

We chose to use JBL component speakers for the Peugeot's front end, mainly because the six-in mid driver will fit in the door, and the tweeters can be mounted well forward on the A-pillars. This lifts the sound and makes it seem like it's well in front of you, where it should be. After all, your ears are designed to pick up sounds from in front of you, so let's put 'em there.

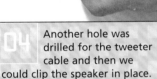

04 Another hole was drilled for the tweeter cable and then we could clip the speaker in place.

05 This small rubber pad was fitted to the back of the trim, presumably to stop anything rattling underneath it. We re-attached it after we'd screwed the tweeter into place, so that it could keep doing its vital job.

06 Here's the driver's side tweeter in position, where it looks pretty discreet, but sounds wicked.

The crossover units were hidden under the dash on each side. Care has to be taken when tightening the terminal screws onto the wiring so that there are no stray strands of wire that **07** could possibly short out and cause damage to the rest of the system.

The trim ring around the door release handle clipped off easily enough, but before we could remove the door panel we had to find all the hidden screws. These are Torx-headed, so after you've found out where they are you still need the correct **08** screwdriver bit before you can attack them.

09 We found screws hidden up under the door pull handle. . .

. . . down behind the electric window switch, and behind a small plug on the door **10** pull handle itself.

11 Once all the Torx screws were undone, we just had to remove the speaker and the panel was ready to be unclipped from the door.

12 The next job was to clean up the door panel before we treated it with sound deadening sheet. Before the Dynamat Xtreme was applied, we used a solvent cleaner to get rid of any dirt and dust, so that the sheet would adhere to the door properly and work well.

13 Dynamat Xtreme doesn't need heating up like a lot of sound deadening products, but it does need rolling onto the door skin to get the best bond possible. We used a hardwood wallpaper edge roller to do this, and once we'd rolled the sheet on, we cut out the holes required by the studs for the door panel, so that it would go back on.

The door panel needed a bit of surgery before it was refitted, because it was a bit too tight around the JBL speaker's magnet. It was a quick fix though, and we only had to remove a little lip of plastic so that it cleared the speaker. **14**

Once the door panel was refitted, the Peugeot speaker plug needed removing and then some proper push-on terminals were fitted in place of it so that the new speaker could be coupled up to the existing speaker cable. **15**

Finally, the mid-range unit was refitted and the front speakers were ready to go. And yes, it isn't the right way up, but because the Pug wire was a bit short in the door, that's the only way it goes. **16**

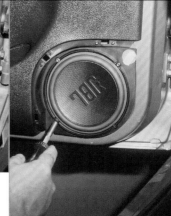

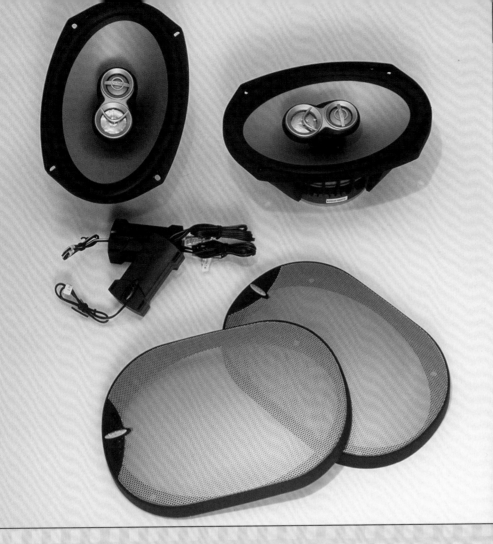

Rear
speakers

Although the Peugeot 306 comes with rear speakers fitted to its removable shelf, they aren't up to much, and in a system like this they would be the weakest link. So it was time we said goodbye to them, and fitted something decent.

To keep things under wraps, we used an Auto Acoustics Stealth shelf. This has raised ribs and, once it's been trimmed, the shelf looks like a standard one. Hide your new speakers underneath it, and no-one knows what you've got pounding away in the back.

There are a couple of things to watch with an MDF shelf, and the main one is the weight. They weigh a ton when they've got speakers in, so make sure you've got it well secured before you go hooning around. Be very careful when screwing the hinge blocks in place, too. Don't strip the wood out or you're in trouble.

Also, Auto Acoustics provide bits of string so that you can tie your shelf to your tailgate and get it to lift the shelf when you open the hatch. Yeah right. Being so heavy, most hatch rams won't support the shelf in the upright position, so we left our bits of string off.

01 We started off by marking the Infinity speakers' required position on the top of the shelf, measuring both sides to get equally spaced holes.

02 Then we marked out the speaker screw holes and drilled them out. We flipped the shelf over, used the screw holes to position the template, and drew the speaker hole on the underside. This was cut out using a jigsaw, and then the underside of the shelf was painted to tidy it up.

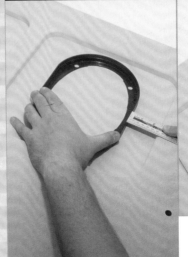

>>

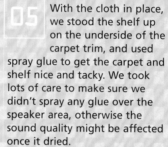

03 When the bottom of the shelf was dry, we took it back to the bench and stapled the acoustic cloth provided over the apertures on the top side of the shelf. This supports the trim that would be covering the speakers.

04 The cloth needs stretching pretty tight so that it doesn't allow any sag, otherwise you'll see an outline of the speakers as time goes on.

05 With the cloth in place, we stood the shelf up on the underside of the carpet trim, and used spray glue to get the carpet and shelf nice and tacky. We took lots of care to make sure we didn't spray any glue over the speaker area, otherwise the sound quality might be affected once it dried.

Once the glue was dry enough, we lowered the shelf onto the carpet, and then flipped it back over to smooth the carpet into place. This needs to be done steadily to stretch the carpet a little so that it follows the ridges in the shelf, but with a bit of work you soon have a shelf that looks just like Peugeot made it.

10 . . . and then tidied the wiring up using P clips along the front edge of the shelf. The quick release Neutrik connector was fitted to the leads and the job was finished.

11 Fitting the Neutrik plug and socket was easy enough, but we did one on the bench so that you could get a better look at it.

12 Job one is to crimp the four supplied spade terminals to the wires that go to the amplifier, and put them onto the socket. The terminals in both bits of the Neutrik are marked so that you can keep the wiring correctly lined up.

13 The plug requires a bit more work, but is still easy. Unscrew the blue collar from the plug and it falls apart. Solder the four small ferrules onto your speaker wires . . .

06 Once the main part of the shelf was covered, we did the rear lip, and then turned it over to do the bottom.

07 This needed a bit of care to get it to look neat around the corners, but if you use a sharp knife and straight edge, you should have no difficulty getting results like this.

08 Once the carpet was sorted out, we fitted the plastic hinge pins to the shelf using the supplied screws. Be very careful when doing this because the screws are easy to strip out of the MDF shelf, and if you do that you won't be able to get the shelf to locate properly in the car.

09 The next job was to attach the Infinity speakers to the pilot holes we'd already drilled. This didn't take long, but fitting the outboard crossovers that came with them needed a bit more thought. In the end we hot glued them into position alongside the speakers . . .

14 . . . and then begin to assemble the plug. Once you've threaded your speaker wire through the collar, and the correct size of clamp ring, insert each wire into its correct socket, and tighten the small screw onto the ferrule.

15 After you've done that, you can push the bits together, and screw the blue collar down onto the plug body.

16 It should look like this when you've finished.

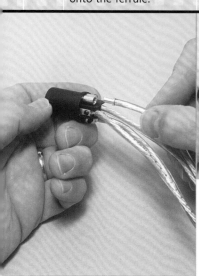 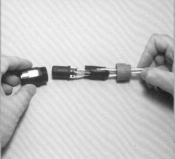 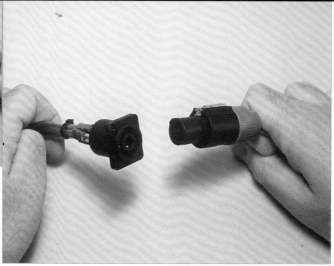

Wiring-up

Getting the wiring-up right means decent music, no fire hazards, and no weird noises coming from the speakers. Getting it wrong can mean your car goes up in smoke. Don't laugh, it does happen.

When you're running amplifier power wire, you must use a fuse near the battery, and you must use a grommet to protect the wire where it goes through the bulkhead. You must also keep it as far as possible from any of the car's wiring to stop any aggro with airbags, seatbelt tensioners and things like that. The signal cable from head unit to amplifier needs running away from the car's wiring as well as the amplifier power cable, so that it doesn't pick up any interference. Speaker wire is probably the least affected by this, but it's still a good idea to keep it away from the car's looms just in case.

01 The Peugeot's power cabling started with a connection to the main battery terminal, and a fuseholder was fitted as close to the battery as possible. A few cable ties held the wire neatly out of the way and stopped it trailing into anything that might damage it. 'Always leave the fuse out until you've finished doing the wiring, then there's no chance of shorting out anything vital.

02 The area that gave most trouble when wiring a 306 was actually getting the wire into the car. There were no suitable grommets to stick our new wire through, so we had to drill our own hole.

We found a flat area next to the air conditioning drain tube, and drilled a pilot hole there to check it was in the right place. Once we were satisfied that this was going to do the job, the hole was **03** opened up to take the grommet supplied with the power cable.

When the cable was in place, we covered the grommet with black silicon sealer to make sure that no water could get in. When you do this you must use a grommet like we did to prevent the wire chafing through and causing problems. **04** Silicone sealer on its own won't do.

The centre console had to be removed to get the wiring to run **05** properly.

It's held in by a couple of concealed screws and nuts, and you should make sure you've got them out of the way **06** before you go heaving on anything and break it.

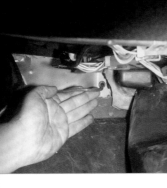

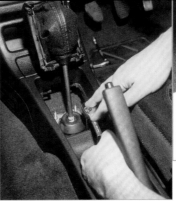

07 This shows how the wiring was laid out along the 306's floor. We kept the cables apart as much as we could, both from each other and the car's wiring looms. This helps to keep out any nasty noises, and stops any possibility of the stereo interfering with any vehicle systems.

08 The terminals we used on the amplifier wiring were crimped on, starting with wire strippers like this to get rid of the wire's plastic insulation.

09 These special crimpers made squeezing the terminals onto the bare wire dead easy. Pliers like this are available at some decent motor accessory shops and car audio stores, so try and get the right tool for the job.

10 To keep things looking neat and safe we used heatshrink tubing over the joints. We could have used a heatgun to shrink the tubing, but we had a gas-powered soldering iron so we used that instead. A quick blast of hot air from the iron's exhaust was all that was needed to give the desired effect, but be careful not to touch the tip directly to the heatshrink, or you'll melt it.

11 We had to cheat slightly with the Pug's front speaker wiring because it ran through a multipin plug that stopped us easily running new speaker wire into the door. Instead, we joined the wire from the mid-range crossover feed onto the front speaker wire at the head unit. We soldered this joint for the best connection, but if you've never soldered, you need to know how to do it.

12 When you need to join two wires, bare the ends back enough so that you can twist them together to give a strong join like these two here. If you're using heatshrink tube to protect the joint, don't forget to slide it onto the wire before you start soldering or you won't be able to get it on afterwards.

13 Once your iron is stinking hot, melt a dab of solder onto the tip and then place this against the joint area to heat it up. After a few seconds you can apply the solder wire to the iron tip and watch the solder flood through the joint. You need to end up with a smooth joint like this one, rather than two pieces of wire with a round blob of solder sitting on top of them. Keep the iron in place until the solder flows or you won't have a good connection.

14 To finish things off, a quick blast of hot air on the heat shrink makes a tidy joint that won't come apart in a hurry. If you haven't got heatshrink tube, insulation tape will do OK, just make sure it covers all the bare wire.

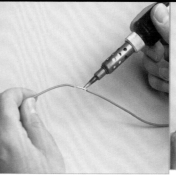

Engines

Faster, faster!

We're not to going to tell you how to
supercharge your 306, or how to drop in the V6
from the 406 Coupe - that'd take a whole book
on its own. If you're that serious, check out one
of the many specialists around the country. What
we tell you how to do is fit an induction kit and
generally sort what's already there. Servicing
ensures your motor's sweet to start with. Get it
tuned professionally after doing each job to get
the most out of your mods.

Replacement engine

If your engine's past it, or you want a simpler
route to more performance, how about an
engine change? The trick is, of course, to make
sure the "new" engine's better than the old one
- some "recon" engines might actually be worse!

If your car's done a huge mileage, a newer lower-mileage motor
will make a big difference. As long as the new engine's the same
size as the old one, it won't affect the insurance - all you do is tell
the DVLA, and they'll update the car's registration document.

Fitting a larger engine should be an easy enough upgrade, but
this time, the insurance must be told, and it's likely they'll insist on
a full engineer's report (these aren't especially expensive - look one
up in the Yellow Pages). However, by the time you've fitted the new
larger engine, your car is now officially "modified" and your
premium is more than a standard larger-engined 306 would be!

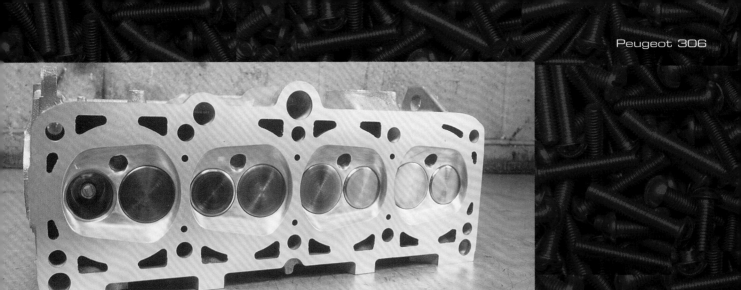

Breathe easier

One of the simplest items to fit, the replacement air filter element has been around for years. It has recently been overtaken in popularity by the induction kit (which is generally only available for fuel injection engines).

The idea of these items is to increase the flow of air into the engine, to help the engine to "breathe", but they can upset the air/fuel mixture and cause poor running. Having the car set-up afterwards on a rolling road is pretty much essential to make the mods actually work. On some fuel injection engines, feeding in extra air will "fool" the injection system into providing more fuel - ultimately, this will increase performance a bit, but will greatly increase fuel consumption and lead to an over-rich mixture, which could cause the car to fail the MOT.

Once you've fitted your new filter or induction kit, even if you don't take the car to a rolling road for setting up, at least take it to a garage and have the emissions checked - any minor adjustments should ensure that the engine will still tick over okay, and should pass an MOT.

An introduction to induction

An aftermarket air filter or induction kit will probably the first thing on your shopping list, after your big-bore back box. The idea of a filter or induction kit is to increase the flow of air into the engine, to help it "breathe" more easily. But surely the original induction system is designed to perfectly suit the engine?. Of course it is - the standard system gives the best possible results achievable, whilst ensuring the incoming air is completely clean, and the stringent regs for noise and emission levels are met. Car makers have to make compromises - an aftermarket supplier's design brief is power, power and more power!

The theory behind an aftermarket air filter element or induction kit is that they allow more air to enter the intake manifold. Fuel and air must be mixed at a specific ratio (around 15 parts air to one of fuel) for optimum performance. Bearing this in mind, it follows that the more air you draw in, the more fuel you can supply with it. More air and fuel mixture equals a bigger charge entering the combustion chamber. A bigger charge equals a bigger bang, which results in a greater power output.

If that's the case then, why don't I just remove the air filter altogether, we hear you ask. True, that would result in maximum possible airflow, but with drastic consequences. The air filter is there to remove all the particles, large and small, and ensure a supply of "clean" air to the engine. Remove the filter element and your engine will end up swallowing dirt, dust, insects, rocks and maybe even small furry mammals. None of these will do anything to improve the combustion process, and will result in wear and damage to your engine. Not a great problem if you're running a touring car around Silverstone for 30 laps on a Sunday afternoon, but a bit more of a worry if you want to keep the engine happy and healthy for a few years to come.

As well as wanting more air, it is equally important that the air supply is cool. Cool air is denser than warm air, which is another important factor in increasing intake air capacity and therefore power. The original air filter intake is at the front of the car for this very reason.

Induction kit

Above all the performance mods you can make on an engine, and that means any engine from a standard 1.1 to a hi-spec turbo 2-litre, a high-flow air filter is the one addition that will always net results. The bonus is that it's also one of the easiest modifications to make, and while manufacturers have made intakes more complex, the kits have kept up with them so you can still buy everything you need in one go.

Being one of the biggest names in air filter technology, K&N have always had a reputation for high quality, high-flow kits, and even with the amount of names in the market today, they still produce one of the best purchases you can make for your modified car.

We chose their induction kit for our 306 which goes way beyond a simple filter, incorporating the pipework necessary to feed your engine with cold air. So follow our tips for a better looking engine bay, a more impressive induction roar and, most importantly, more power under your right foot.

01 The K&N Induction Kit comprises a cone filter, new breather pipes, a venturi section (shown with the Jubilee clip on it) all the cable ties necessary plus a cold air intake which we couldn't use, but more on that later.

02 The standard intake pipe takes in cold air from the grille area, which is a good start.

03 Removing the standard pipework is simply a matter of cutting the cable ties which hold it in position.

04 Next, lift out the pipework and store it. You can see that with the bends and reduction in pipe diameter, the section is not suited to high air flow.

05 To remove the air box you first have to take our this inlet air temperature sensor, which is re-used in the K&N kit.

06 Unplug the sensor wire and tuck it to one side.

07 Next you can unscrew the sensor and put it one side for the moment.

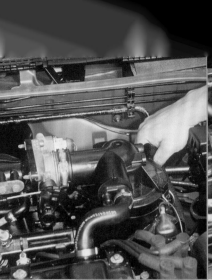

08 Pull off the large breather pipe on the rear of the air box. This will refit into the K&N cone filter.

09 Remove the small breather hose at the front of the air box. This is another pipe that will be refitted in the filter.

10 Using a screwdriver, release the clips which hold the rocker cover breather pipe.

The K&N cone filter needs to have the small front and large rear breather pipes fitted into it (not the breather pipe from the rocker cover). We found it necessary to cut the larger rear pipe back a bit in order for it to fit inside the filter without kinking. Apply a bit of WD-40 to the pipes also, as they're a squeeze to insert.

The intake air temperature sensor screws into the K&N venturi and has to sit as far down into the pipe as possible.

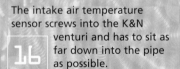

14

15 The filter is positioned with both of the pipes at the bottom, but first the rest of the kit must be fitted.

16

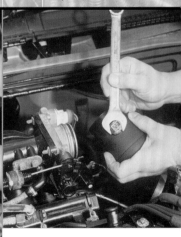

11 Remove the pipe altogether, it won't be re-used as K&N supply a replacement shaped pipe in their kit.

12 Unscrew the Jubilee clip connecting the air box to the throttle body.

13 The air box can be removed now. It's an ugly thing which looks better in the bin than in your car's engine bay. Still, better store it just in case you intend to sell the car standard in the future.

>>

17 Reconnect the sensor wiring.

18 Fit the thinnest Jubilee clip in the K&N kit around the venturi, then fit the venturi to the throttle body, taking care not to unseat the rubber seal on the body neck.

19 Tighten the Jubilee clip only enough so you can still rotate the venturi because it's unlikely to be in exactly the right position just yet.

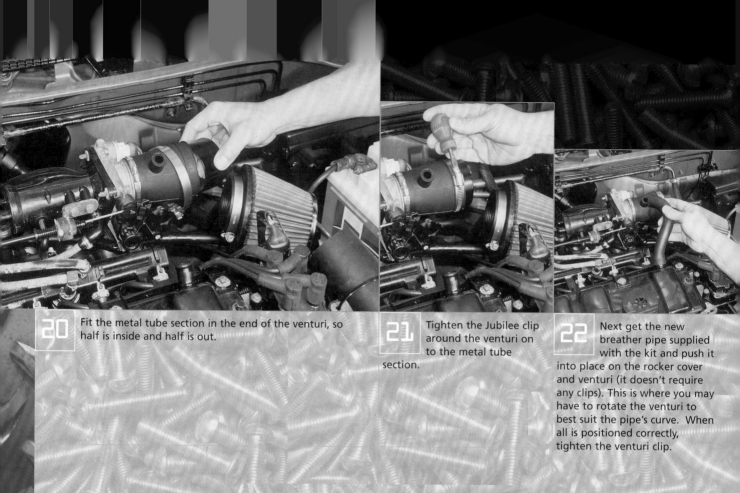

20 Fit the metal tube section in the end of the venturi, so half is inside and half is out.

21 Tighten the Jubilee clip around the venturi on to the metal tube section.

22 Next get the new breather pipe supplied with the kit and push it into place on the rocker cover and venturi (it doesn't require any clips). This is where you may have to rotate the venturi to best suit the pipe's curve. When all is positioned correctly, tighten the venturi clip.

26 Drill the K&N-supplied intake pipe extension and cable tie this to the intake pipe. Ordinarily this would sit down in the grille area, being force fed with cold air as the car moves along. This is where we ran into a problem.

27 Our car had twin electric fans mounted on the front of the radiator, which meant there was no room for the intake pipe extension. We tried cutting it down, but it wouldn't work as there simply wasn't the space even for a shorter version.

28 As the intake pipe draws in cold air from the high-pressure grille area, we chucked the extension pipe back in the K&N box and made do with the standard part, which just meant bolting it back into place.

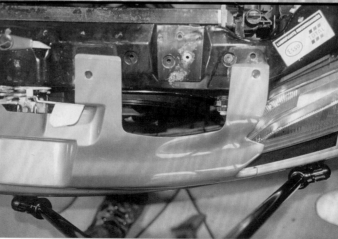

23 You can now push the filter into place but don't push via the element area, only by the chrome end plate where the K&N logo is.

24 Tighten the Jubilee clip, making sure the filter is sitting square on the metal tube. This finishes the work here.

25 You can now switch to the pipework necessary to supply the filter with cold air. Remove the intake pipe, which directs air from the grille area, and drill it with three 3mm holes, one on the narrow side and two either side of centre on the main flat part (all as per the K&N instructions).

Cable tie the concertina pipe back in position (actually this doesn't need removing in the first place, but we assumed it did so had cut its cable tie).

29

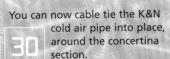

30 You can now cable tie the K&N cold air pipe into place, around the concertina section.

31 The cold air pipe also needs to be cable tied to the engine to hold it steady.

32 Your engine bay should now look much better. Time to crank the car up and feel the difference.

More show than go

All show and no go, yes, but you can't deny they look good. For those of you who like to spend time admiring what's under the bonnet, there's a wide range of accessories to tidy up and customise your engine compartment. Here's a rough guide to a few of the options available.

Customised rocker/cam cover

Another easy-fit item which is very effective at improving the appearance of your engine compartment. Covers only seem to be readily available for the 8-valve engines, but there's nothing to stop you spraying any cover you want - just remember to use heat-resistant paint if you want the finished result to last.

Battery and ECU covers

Simple to fit and very effective. Replace the naff plastic ECU cover with a more stylish alloy/carbon cover and fit a matching cover to the battery or fuse box for an altogether more co-ordinated look. Especially when combined with a matching rocker/cam cover. You could even spray some items with heat-resistant paint.

One thing to be wary of though - if you're installing a metal battery cover, ensure the battery terminals are sufficiently insulated and in no danger of 'shorting' out on the cover. A direct 'short' via a metal battery cover could result in your battery quite literally exploding and emitting a shower of battery acid over anything in its vicinity, ie. the engine compartment and quite possibly you. Nasty business.

We could go on but you get the picture. If the products you want aren't available to buy, why not colour-code the standard items (see painting information in "Body and styling").

HT leads

Not a great deal of point in changing your HT leads, because they're not the most visible thing under the bonnet - and that's assuming your 306's even got any. Diesels, of course, are a bit light in the HT lead department. Don't be sold by claims that new leads will enhance your car's performance, either - unless the old leads are shot, you really won't see any improvement.

New leads are only an option on early models with a separate ignition coil and HT leads - some later petrol models are fitted with "plug top" ignition coils of one sort or another. Lift the bonnet to see what you've got. If you can't see a separate ignition coil (on the left-hand end of the head) or any HT leads on the spark plugs (fitted to the rear of the cylinder head) you've got "plug top" ignition coils, and it's game over on the mods front.

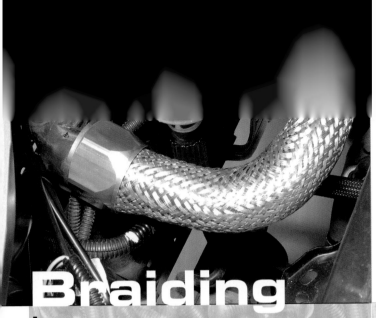

Braiding hoses

Turning your engine bay into something resembling that of a racing machine should only be done when the engine's completely cold to start with - like first thing in the morning, not when you've just got back from the cruise. The smell of burning flesh is never pleasant, especially when it's yours.

Depending on which hoses you decide to treat, you could be removing ones containing hot coolant or fuel, and you don't play games with either, so be smart. If you're planning to braid your fuel lines, disconnect the hoses very carefully - have some rags wrapped around the pipes, so you don't spray high-pressure fuel everywhere.

01 First step is to remove your chosen hose. On our 306, we wanted to braid the radiator top hose, which meant removing the air intake first. Peugeot tend to use spring-type clips, best released using pliers, but you might find Jubilee clips. If the hose is stuck, be careful how you free it, or you could snap the pipe stub underneath. This sort of thing can really ruin your day.

02 Unroll your braiding, then expand it to the right size using a suitable object like a broom handle or screwdriver.

When you're sure the hose is fully onto its fitting, tighten the hose clip securely. Fit the other end of the hose and tighten the clip in place. If any of the end fittings rattle annoyingly, you can put a stop to it by packing the fittings with silicone. Don't forget to top up the coolant before heading out.

03 Once the braiding's roughly the right size, you can slip your pipe in.

04 Trim off the excess, then smooth out the braiding round the bends, as it tends to gather up and look naff otherwise.

05 Slide a new Jubilee clip into an end fitting, then fit one end of the pipe in place. The hose clip is supposed to slide right up inside the end fitting, so it clamps the hose, the end of the braiding, and the end fitting (even when tight, the end fittings are still sometimes loose, though).

06

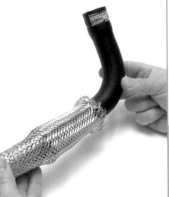

Attention!
If you are braiding coolant hoses, feel them first to make sure they're cold. Have a bowl ready to catch the coolant. Antifreeze is poisonous despite its sweet smell, and will make a mess of your paintwork if you douse the engine bay and front wings with it.

Although not as effective as a full-uprated exhaust system, a back box alone will make a car sound and look nicer.

Make sure you check when you're buying that it can be fitted to a standard system - you'll probably need something called a reducing sleeve for a decent fit, which is a cone-shaped section designed to bridge the difference between your small-diameter pipe and the larger-diameter silencer. Try to get a back box designed for your car, but if you go for a universal system measure your standard pipe as accurately as possible, or you'll have problems trying to get a decent seal between the old and new bits.

13 Exhausts

Fashion has entered the aftermarket exhaust scene, with different rear pipe designs going in and out of style. Everyone's done the upswept twin-pipe DTM style pipes, while an emerging trend is simply the "bigger the better" look.

You will begin to see some useful power gains if you go for the complete performance exhaust system, rather than just the back box. Like the factory-fit system, the sports silencer will only work at its best if combined with the front pipe and, better still, the four-branch manifold it was designed for. Many aftermarket systems need careful fitting to stop them resonating or banging away underneath. A sports rear box alone shouldn't attract an increased insurance premium, but a full system could.

All 306s were fitted with a catalytic converter (or "cat"), and you're no doubt aware that the cat acts like a restrictor in the exhaust, inhibiting the gas flow and sapping some engine power (maybe 5 to 10%). Some companies market replacement systems which do away with the cat (a de-cat pipe), and these will have a useful effect. While fitting a de-cat pipe is an easy and proven route to more power, the car won't be legal on the road without its cat (it's not MOT-able) which could prove a bit embarrassing if you have an accident while the de-cat pipe's in place.

Exhaust rear box

Peco's line of stainless steel rear boxes not only look the business, they sound throaty but aren't too loud. The unit comes **01** with a bracket to hang the box in the factory position.

The standard rear box is tucked away behind the rear valance, hence it can't be seen which is **02** probably a blessing given the tailpipe's puny size.

If there's one area where manufacturers consistently fail to produce the goods on the styling of their vehicles it's on the exhaust tailpipe. Sure, there are a few exceptions on more expensive cars, but generally the size of most tailpipes and ugly bulk of a silencer behind it leave a lot to be desired. But there are loads of aftermarket backboxes to remedy the situation, and most are dead easy to fit in just a few hours.

There's also a massive choice of type and shape of pipe – we've seen them all done on Peugeots, and not all look right. A twin DTM style pipe is cool, though that style is getting a bit long in the tooth now. Anything square is a definite no-no because of the Peugeot's rounded rump and edges. What looks best on the 306 is either an oval pipe or a single large round one. With the body kit we were fitting having space for up to a 4-inch whopper, we chose to go with a 3-inch pipe with a rolled edge, from Peco.

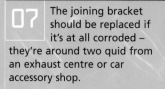

07 The joining bracket should be replaced if it's at all corroded – they're around two quid from an exhaust centre or car accessory shop.

08 The bracket should be put into place and the nuts just hand-tightened for the moment.

09 It's a good idea to buy replacement exhaust hangers, these ones being beefed-up for a more steady fixing, given the skinny nature of the factory items.

03 To remove the factory unit you have just two bolts to undo on the bracket which joins it to the rest of the system. Being as our car was a few years old, the bracket was rusted solid, but luckily it virtually fell apart after a bit of gentle persuasion and swearing.

04 Removing the standard unit is simple – once the bracket's off there's just the rubber hangers left to contend with.

05 We found the bracket which came with the Peco unit had one arm which was pointing the wrong way. We tried bending it 180 degrees but, being stainless steel and consequently very hard, it snapped clean off.

06 A trip to a local welders saw the arm back on, this time the right way around.

10 The pipe where the back box joins must be scraped clean of surface rust and old exhaust joint paste.

11 Fresh exhaust joint paste should be spread around to form a good seal. This stuff remains soft until it gets hot, therefore it won't set while you're putting the box into place, only when the engine is fired up.

12 It's helpful to install one rubber hanger first, to take the weight off the 'box, which becomes awkward when you're lying under a car.

13 With both rubbers on and the joining bracket tightened around 50%, start the car up and check for leaks. There was one on our joining bracket, so we simply loosened the box bracket and rotated the unit until it was better seated on the join.

14 Very business like. Three inches fat and with a deep burble, the Peco unit will give your Pug the look and sound of a performer. Ours should fit neatly in the new Ecosse rear bumper we're planning to use, but if you're sticking with the stock rear bumper it's likely you'll have to modify the bodywork or use an aluminium plate heat shield.

Safety and tools

Safety

We all know that working on your car can be dangerous - and we're not talking about the danger of losing your street cred by fitting naff alloys or furry dice! Okay, so you'd be hard-pushed to injure yourself fitting some cool floor mats or a tax disc holder, but tackle more-serious mods, and you could be treading dangerous ground. Let's be honest - we have to put this safety section in to cover ourselves, but now it's in, it would be nice if you read it…

Burning/scalding

The only way you'll really burn yourself is if your car's just been running - avoid this, and you won't get burned. Easy, eh? Otherwise, you risk burns from any hot parts of the engine (and especially the exhaust - if you've got one, the cat runs very hot), or from spilling hot coolant if you undo the radiator hoses or filler cap, as you might when you're braiding hoses.

Fire

Sadly, there's several ways your car could catch fire, when you think about it. You've got a big tank full of fuel (and other flammable liquids about, like brake fluid), together with electrics - some of which run to very high voltages. If you smoke too, this could be even worse for your health than you thought.

a Liquid fuel is flammable. Fuel vapour can explode - don't smoke, or create any kind of spark, if there's fuel vapour (fuel smell) about.

b Letting fuel spill onto a hot engine is dangerous, but brake fluid spills go up even more readily. Respect is due with brake fluid, which also attacks paintwork and plastics - wash off with water.

c Fires can also be started by careless modding involving the electrical system. It's possible to overload (and overheat) existing wiring by tapping off too many times for new live feeds. Not insulating bare wires or connections can lead to short-circuits, and the sparks or overheated wiring which results can start a fire. Always investigate any newly-wired-in kit which stops working, or which keeps blowing fuses - those wires could already be smouldering…

Crushing

Having your car land on top of you is no laughing matter, and it's a nasty accident waiting to happen if you risk using dodgy old jacks, bricks, and other means of lifting/supporting your car. Please don't.

Your standard vehicle jack is for emergency roadside use only - a proper trolley jack and a set of axle stands won't break the overdraft, and might save broken bones. Don't buy a cheap trolley jack, and don't expect a well-used secondhand one to be perfect, either - when the hydraulic seals start to fail, a trolley jack will drop very fast; this is why you should always have decent stands in place under the car as well.

Steering, suspension & brakes

Screwing up any one of these on your car, through badly-fitted mods, could land you and others in hospital or worse. Nuff said? It's always worth getting a mate, or a friendly garage, to check over what you've just fitted (or even what you've just had fitted, in some cases - not all "pro" fitters are perfect!). Pay attention to tightening vital nuts and bolts properly - buy or borrow a torque wrench.

To be absolutely sure, take your newly-modded machine to a friendly MOT tester (if there is such a thing) - this man's your ultimate authority on safety, after all. Even if he's normally a pain once a year, he could save your life. Think it over.

Even properly-fitted mods can radically alter the car's handling - and not always for the better. Take a few days getting used to how the car feels before showing off.

Wheels

Don't take liberties fitting wheels. Make sure the wheels have the right stud/bolt hole pattern for your car, and that the wheel nuts/bolts are doing their job. Bolts which are too long might catch on your brakes (especially rear drums) - too short, and, well, the wheels are just waiting to fall off. Not nice. Also pay attention to the bolt heads or wheel nuts - some are supposed to have large tapered washers fitted, to locate properly in the wheel. If the nuts/bolts "pull through" the wheel when tightened, the wheel's gonna fall off, isn't it?

Asbestos

Only likely to be a major worry when working on, or near, your brakes. That black dust that gets all over your alloys comes from your brake pads, and it may contain asbestos. Breathing in asbestos dust can lead to a disease called asbestosis (inflammation of the lungs - very nasty indeed), so try not to inhale brake dust when you're changing your pads or discs.

Airbags

Unless you run into something at high speed, the only time an airbag will enter your life is when you change your steering wheel for something more sexy, and have to disable the airbag in the process. Pay attention to all the precautionary advice given in our text, and you'll have no problems.

One more thing - don't tap into the airbag wiring to run any extra electrical kit. Any mods to the airbag circuit could set it off unexpectedly.

Exhaust gases

Even on cars with cats, exhaust fumes are still potentially lethal. Don't work in an unventilated garage with the engine running. When fitting new exhaust bits, be sure that there's no gas leakage from the joints. When modifying in the tailgate area, note that exhaust gas can get sucked into the car through badly-fitting tailgate seals/joints (or even through your rear arches, if they've been trimmed so much there's holes into the car).

Tools

In writing this book, we've assumed you already have a selection of basic tools - screwdrivers, socket set, spanners, hammer, sharp knife, power drill. Any unusual extra tools you might need are mentioned in the relevant text. Torx and Allen screws are often found on trim panels, so a set of keys of each type is a wise purchase.

From a safety angle, always buy the best tools you can afford - or if you must use cheap ones, remember that they can break under stress or unusual usage (and we've all got the busted screwdrivers to prove it!).

DO Wear goggles when using power tools.

DO Keep loose clothing/long hair away from moving engine parts.

DO Take off watches and jewellery when working on electrics.

DO Keep the work area tidy - stops accidents and losing parts.

DON'T Rush a job, or take stupid short-cuts.

DON'T Use the wrong tools for the job, or ones which don't fit.

DON'T Let kids or pets play around your car when you're working.

DON'T Work entirely alone under a car that's been jacked up.

Legal modding?
No such thing!!

The harsh & painful truth

The minute you start down the road to a modified motor, you stand a good chance of being in trouble with the Man. It seems like there's almost nothing worthwhile you can do to your car, without breaking some sort of law. So the answer's not to do it at all, then? Well, no, but let's keep it real.

There's this bunch of vehicle-related regulations called Construction & Use. It's a huge set of books, used by the car manufacturers and the Department of Transport among others, and it sets out in black and white all the legal issues that could land you in trouble. It's the ultimate authority for modifying, in theory. But few people (and even fewer policemen) know all of it inside-out, and it's forever being updated and revised, so it's not often enforced to the letter at the roadside - just in court. Despite the existence of C & U, in trying to put together any guide to the law and modifying, it quickly becomes clear that almost everything's a "grey area", with no-one prepared to go on record and say what is okay to modify and what's not. Well, brilliant. So if there's no fixed rules (in the real world), how are you meant to live by them? In the circumstances, all we can promise to do is help to make sense of nonsense…

Avoiding roadside interviews

Why do some people get pulled all the time, and others hardly ever? It's often all about attitude. We'd all like to be free to drive around "in yer face", windows down, system full up, loud exhaust bellowing, sparks striking, tyres squealing - but - nothing is a bigger "come-on" to the boys in blue than "irresponsible" driving like this. Rest assured, if your motor's anywhere near fully sorted, the coppers will find something they can nick you for, when they pull you over - it's a dead cert. Trying not to wind them up too much before this happens (and certainly not once you're stopped) will make for an easier life. There's showing off, and then there's taking the pee. Save it for the next cruise.

The worst thing from your point of view is that, once you've been stopped, it's down to that particular copper's judgement as to whether your car's illegal. If he/she's having a bad day anyway, smart-mouthing-off isn't gonna help your case at all. If you can persuade him/her that you're at least taking on board what's being said, you might be let off with a warning. If it goes further, you'll be reported for an offence - while this doesn't mean you'll end up being prosecuted for it, it ain't good. Some defects (like worn tyres) will result in a so-called "seven-day wonder", which usually means you have to fix whatever's deemed wrong, maybe get the car inspected, and present yourself with the proof at a police station, inside seven days, or face prosecution.

If you can manage to drive reasonably sensibly when the law's about, and can ideally show that you've tried to keep your car legal when you get questioned, you stand a much better chance of enjoying your relationship with your modded beast. This guide is intended to help you steer clear of the more obvious things you could get pulled for. By reading it, you might even be able to have an informed, well-mannered discussion about things legal with the next officer of the law you meet at the side of the road. As in: "Oh really, officer? I was not aware of that. Thank you for pointing it out." Just don't argue with them, that's all…

Documents

The first thing you'll be asked to produce. If you're driving around without tax, MOT or insurance, we might as well stop now, as you won't be doing much more driving of anything after just one pull.

Okay, so you don't normally carry all your car-related documents with you - for safety, you've got them stashed carefully at home, haven't you? But carrying photocopies of your licence, MOT and insurance certificate is a good idea. While they're not legally-binding absolute proof, producing these in a roadside check might mean you don't have to produce the real things at a copshop later in the week. Shows a certain responsibility, and confidence in your own legality on the road, too. In some parts of the country, it's even said to be a good idea to carry copies of any receipts for your stereo gear - if there's any suspicion about it being stolen (surely not), some coppers have been known to confiscate it (or the car it's in) on the spot!

Number plates

One of the simplest mods, and one of the easiest to spot (and prove) if you're a copper. Nowadays, any changes made to the standard approved character font (such as italics or fancy type), spacing, or size of the plate constitutes an offence. Remember too that if you've moved the rear plate from its original spot (like from the tailgate recess, during smoothing) it still has to be properly lit at night. You're unlikely to even buy an illegal plate now, as the companies making them are also liable for prosecution if you get stopped. It's all just something else to blame on speed cameras - plates have to be easy for them to shoot, and modding yours suggests you're trying to escape a speeding conviction (well, who isn't?).

Getting pulled for an illegal plate is for suckers - you're making it too easy for them. While this offence only entails a small fine and confiscation of the plates, you're drawing unwelcome police attention to the rest of your car. Not smart. At all.

Sunstrips and tints

The sunstrip is now an essential item for any modded motor, but telling Mr Plod you had to fit one is no defence if you've gone a bit too far. The sunstrip should not be so low down the screen that it interferes with your ability to see out. Is this obvious? Apparently not. As a guide, if the strip's so low your wiper(s) touch it, it's too low. Don't try fitting short wiper blades to get round this - the police aren't as stupid as that, and you could get done for wipers that don't clear a sufficient area of the screen. Push it so far, and no further!

Window tinting is a trickier area. It seems you can have up to a 25% tint on a windscreen, and up to 30% on all other glass - but how do you measure this? Er. And what do you do if your glass is tinted to start with? Er, probably nothing. Of course you can buy window film in various "darknesses", from not-very-dark to "ambulance-black", but being able to buy it does not make it legal for road use (most companies cover themselves by saying "for show use only"). Go for just a light smoke on the side and rear glass, and you'd have to be unlucky to get done for it. If you must fit really dark tints, you're safest doing the rear side windows only.

Some forces now have a light meter to test light transmission through glass at the roadside - fail this, and it's a big on-the-spot fine.

Single wiper conversion

Not usually a problem, and certainly not worth a pull on its own, but combine a big sunstrip with a short wiper blade, and you're just asking for trouble. Insufficient view of the road ahead. There's also the question of whether it's legal to have the arm parking vertically, in the centre of the screen, as it obscures your vision. Probably not legal, then - even if it looks cool. Unfortunately, the Man doesn't do cool.

Lights

Lights of all kinds have to be one of the single biggest problem areas in modifying, and the police are depressingly well-informed. Most people make light mods a priority, whether it's Morette conversions for headlights or Lexus-style rear clusters. If they fit alright, and work, what's the problem?

First off, don't bother with any lights which aren't fully UK-legal - it's just too much hassle. Being "E-marked" only makes them legal in Europe, and most of our Euro-chums drive on the right. One of our project cars ended up with left-hand-drive rear clusters, and as a result, had no rear reflectors and a rear foglight on the wrong side (should be on the right). Getting stopped for not having rear reflectors would be a bit harsh, but why risk it, even to save a few quid?

Once you've had any headlight mods done (other than light brows) always have the beam alignment checked - it's part of the MOT, after all. The same applies to any front fogs or spots you've fitted (the various points of law involved here are too many to mention - light colour, height, spacing, operation with main/dipped headlights - ask at an MOT centre before fitting, and have them checked out after fitting).

If Plod's really having a bad day, he might even question the legality of your new blue headlight bulbs - are they too powerful? Keeping the bulb packaging in the glovebox might be a neat solution here (60/55W max).

Many modders favour spraying rear light clusters to make them look trick, as opposed to replacing them - but there's trouble in store here, too. One of the greyest of grey areas is - how much light tinting is too much? The much-talked-about but not-often-seen "common sense" comes into play here. Making your lights so dim that they're reduced to a feeble red/orange glow is pretty dim itself. If you're spraying, only use proper light-tinting spray, and not too many coats of that. Colour-coding lights with ordinary spray paint is best left to a pro sprayer or bodyshop (it can be done by mixing lots of lacquer with not much paint, for instance). Tinted lights are actually more of a problem in daylight than at night, so check yours while the sun's out.

Lastly, two words about neons. Oh, dear. It seems that neons of all kinds have now been deemed illegal for road use (and that's

interior ones as well as exteriors, which have pretty much always been a no-no). If you fit neons inside, make sure you rig in a switch so you can easily turn them off when the law arrives - or don't drive around with them on (save it for when you're parked up). Distracts other road users, apparently.

ICE

Jungle massive, or massive public nuisance? The two sides of the ICE argument in a nutshell. If you've been around the modding scene for any length of time, you'll already know stories of people who've been done for playing car stereos too loud. Seems some local authorities now have by-laws concerning "music audible from outside a vehicle", and hefty fines if you're caught. Even where this isn't the case, and assuming a dB meter isn't on hand to prove the offence of "excessive noise", the police can still prosecute for "disturbing the peace" - on the basis of one officer's judgement of the noise level. If a case is proved, you could lose your gear. Whoops. Seems we're back to "do it - but don't over-do it" again. If you really want to demo your system, pick somewhere a bit less public (like a quiet trading estate, after dark) or go for safety in numbers (at a cruise).

Big alloys/tyres

One of the first things to go on any lad's car, sexy alloys are right at the heart of car modifying. So what'll interest the law?

Well, the first thing every copper's going to wonder is - are the wheels nicked? He'd need a good reason to accuse you, but this is another instance where having copies of receipts might prove useful.

Otherwise, the wheels mustn't rub on, or stick out from, the arches - either of these will prove to be a problem if you get stopped. And you don't need to drive a modded motor to get done for having bald tyres…

Lowered suspension

Of course you have to lower your car, to have any hope of street cred. But did you know it's actually an offence to cause damage to the road surface, if your car's so low (or your mates so lardy) that it grounds out? Apparently so! Never mind what damage it might be doing to your exhaust, or the brake/fuel lines under the car - you can actually get done for risking damage to the road. Well, great. What's the answer? Once you've lowered the car, load it up with your biggest mates, and test it over roads you normally use - or else find a route into town that avoids all speed bumps. If you've got coilovers, you'll have an easier time tuning out the scraping noises.

Remember that your new big-bore exhaust or backbox must be hung up well enough that it doesn't hit the deck, even if you haven't absolutely slammed your car on the floor. At night, leaving a trail of sparks behind is a bit of a giveaway…

Exhausts

One of the easiest-to-fit performance upgrades, and another essential item if you want to be taken seriously on the street. Unless your chosen pipe/system is just too damn loud, you'd be very unlucky to get stopped for it, but if you will draw attention this way, you could be kicking yourself later.

For instance - have you in fact fitted a home-made straight-through pipe, to a car which used to have a "cat"? By drawing Plod's attention with that extra-loud system, he could then ask you to get the car's emissions tested - worse, you could get pulled for a "random" roadside emissions check. Fail this (and you surely will), and you could be right in the brown stuff. Even if you re-convert the car back to stock for the MOT, you'll be illegal on the road (and therefore without insurance) whenever your loud pipe's on. Still sound like fun, or would you be happier with just a back box?

It's also worth mentioning that your tailpipe mustn't stick out beyond the very back of the car, or in any other way which might be dangerous to pedestrians. Come on - you were a ped once!

Bodykits

The popular bodykits for the UK market have all passed the relevant tests, and are fully-approved for use on the specific vehicles they're intended for. As long as you haven't messed up fitting a standard kit, you should be fine, legally-speaking. The trouble starts when you do your own little mods and tweaks, such as bodging on that huge whale-tail spoiler or front air dam/splitter - it can be argued in some cases that these aren't appropriate on safety grounds, and you can get prosecuted. If any bodywork is fitted so it obscured your lights, or so badly attached that a strong breeze might blow it off, you can see their point. At least there's no such thing as Style Police. Not yet, anyway.

Seats and harnesses

Have to meet the UK safety standards, and must be securely bolted in. That's about it. It should be possible to fasten and release any seat belt or harness with one hand. Given that seat belts are pretty important safety features, it's understandable then that the police don't like to see flimsy alloy rear strut braces used as seat harness mounting points. Any other signs of bodging will also spell trouble. It's unlikely they'd bother with a full safety inspection at the roadside, but they could insist on a full MOT test/engineer's report inside 7 days. It's your life.

While we're on the subject of crash safety, the police also don't like to see sub boxes and amps just lying on the carpet, where the back seat used to be - if it's not anchored down, where are these items gonna end up, in a big shunt? Embedded in you, possibly?

Other mods

We'll never cover everything else here, and the law's always changing anyway, so we're fighting a losing battle in a book like this, but here goes with some other legalistic points we've noted on the way:

a It's illegal to remove side repeaters from front wings, even to create the ultimate smoothed/flushed motor. Sorry.

b All except the most prehistoric cars must have at least one rear foglight. If there's only one, it must be fitted on the right. We've never heard of anyone getting stopped for it, but you must also have a pair of rear reflectors. If your rear clusters ain't got 'em, can you get trendy ones? Er, no.

c Fuel filler caps have to be fitted so there's no danger of fuel spillage, or of excess fumes leaking from the top of the filler neck. This means using an appropriate petrol-resistant sealer (should be supplied in the kit). Oh, and not bodging the job in general seems a good idea. Unlikely to attract a pull, though.

d Front doors have to retain a manual means of opening from outside, even if they've been de-locked for remote locking. This means you can't take off the front door handles, usually. It seems that rear door handles can be removed if you like.

e Tailgates have to have some means of opening, even if it's only from inside, once the lock/handle's been removed. We think it's another safety thing - means of escape in a crash, and all that.

f You have to have at least one exterior mirror, and it must be capable of being adjusted somehow.

g If you fit new fog and spotlights, they actually have to work. No-one fits new lights just for show (or do they?), but if they stop working later when a fuse blows, relay packs up, or the wiring connectors rust up, you'd better fix 'em or remove 'em.

h Pedal extensions must have rubbers fitted on the brake and clutch pedals, and must be spaced sufficiently so there's no chance of hitting two pedals at once. This last bit sounds obvious, but lots of extension sets out there are so hard to fit that achieving this can be rather difficult. Don't get caught out.

i On cars with airbags, if you fit a sports wheel and disconnect the airbag in the process, the airbag warning light will be on permanently. Apart from being annoying, this is also illegal.

j Pace-car strobe lights (or any other flashing lights, apart from indicators) are illegal for road use. Of course.

k Anything else we didn't think of - is probably illegal too. Sorry.

Any questions? Try the MOT Helpline (0845 6005977). Yes, really.

Thanks to Andrew Dare of the Vehicle Inspectorate, Exeter, for his help in steering us through this minefield!

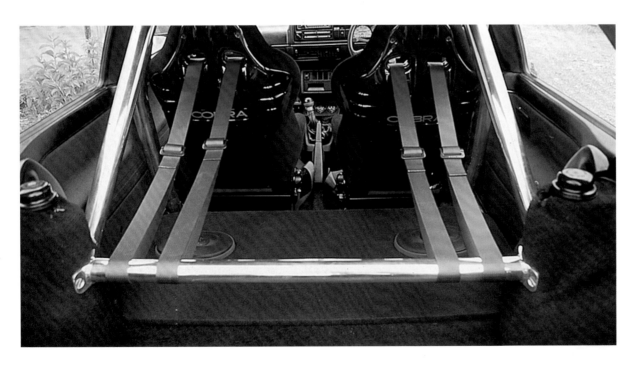

Thanks to:

We gratefully acknowledge all the help and advice offered from the following suppliers, without whom, etc, etc. Many of those credited below went way beyond the call of duty to help us produce this book - you know who you are. Cheers, guys! Roll the credits...

Brown & Geeson Distribution Ltd (Momo)
01268 764411

Corbeau Seats Ltd
01424 854499

CT Autoparts
08000 283 284

Demon Tweeks
01978 663000

Ecosse
01506 516106

Eibach UK
01455 286524

Eurostyling (Foliatec)
0208 987 5519

Halfords
08457 626 625

K & N Filters
01925 636950

LA & RW Piper (car trimming)
01935 851676

Larkspeed
08707 440101

Mille Miglia (UK) Ltd
01626 832222

Performance Parts Direct
01252 517272

Performance Products Ltd
01244 321300

Peter Mayden Components
07002 999 123

R & A Design
01472 811711

RAID
01664 823792

Red Dot Racing Ltd
020 8888 2354

Richbrook
0208 543 7111

Ripspeed at Halfords
0845 609 1259

Safety Devices
01353 724201

Savage, Trillogy
01280 822865

Sedna Service Station
(body styling)
01935 850339

SPAX
01869 244771

Think Automotive
020 8568 1172

Toyo Tyres
01933 411144

A special thankyou to:
Brodie Baxter
Kim Baxter
Andy Butler (ICE words)
Zoë Harrison (ICE pics)
Jon Hill (cover shots)
Ellen and Alan Larkin
Bryn Musselwhite
Diane Paterson
Stewart Smith
Dan White (editor)

Haynes Car Manuals

Model	No.
Alfa Romeo Alfasud/Sprint (74 - 88)	0292
Alfa Romeo Alfetta (73 - 87)	0531
Audi 80 (72 - Feb 79)	0207
Audi 80, 90 (79 - Oct 86) & Coupe (81 - Nov 88)	0605
Audi 80, 90 (Oct 86 - 90) & Coupe (Nov 88 - 90)	1491
Audi 100 (Oct 82 - 90) & 200 (Feb 84 - Oct 89)	0907
Audi 100 & A6 Petrol & Diesel (May 91 - May 97)	3504
Audi A4 (95 - Feb 00)	3575
Austin A35 & A40 (56 - 67)	0118
Austin Allegro 1100, 1300, 1.0, 1.1 & 1.3 (73 - 82)	0164
Austin Healey 100/6 & 3000 (56 - 68)	0049
Austin/MG/Rover Maestro 1.3 & 1.6 (83 - 95)	0922
Austin/MG Metro (80 - May 90)	0718
Austin/Rover Montego 1.3 & 1.6 (84 - 94)	1066
Austin/MG/Rover Montego 2.0 (84 - 95)	1067
Austin/Rover 2.0 litre Diesel Engine (86 - 93)	1857
Bedford CF (69 - 87)	0163
Bedford/Vauxhall Rascal & Suzuki Supercarry (86 - Oct 94)	3015
BMW 1500, 1502, 1600, 1602, 2000 & 2002 (59 - 77)	0240
BMW 316, 320 & 320i (4-cyl) (75 - Feb 83)	0276
BMW 320, 320i, 323i & 325i (6-cyl) (Oct 77 - Sept 87)	0815
BMW 3-Series (Apr 91 - 96)	3210
BMW 3- & 5-Series (sohc)(81 - 91)	1948
BMW 520i & 525e (Oct 81 - June 88)	1560
BMW 525, 528 & 528i (73 - Sept 81)	0632
Citroën 2CV, Ami & Dyane (67 - 90)	0196
Citroën AX Petrol & Diesel (87 - 97)	3014
Citroën BX (83 - 94)	0908
Citroën C15 Van Petrol & Diesel (89 - Oct 98)	3509
Citroën CX (75 - 88)	0528
Citroën Saxo Petrol & Diesel (96 - 01)	3506
Citroën Visa (79 - 88)	0620
Citroën Xantia Petrol & Diesel (93 - 98)	3082
Citroën XM Petrol & Diesel (89 - 98)	3451
Citroën Xsara Petrol & Diesel (97 - Sept 00)	3751
Citroën ZX Diesel (91 - 98)	1922
Citroën ZX Petrol (91 - 98)	1881
Citroën 1.7 & 1.9 litre Diesel Engine (84 - 96)	1379
Fiat 126 (73 - 87)	0305
Fiat 500 (57 - 73)	0090
Fiat Bravo & Brava (95 - 00)	3572
Fiat Cinquecento (93 - 98)	3501
Fiat Panda (81 - 95)	0793
Fiat Punto Petrol & Diesel (94 - Oct 99)	3251
Fiat Regata (84 - 88)	1167
Fiat Tipo (88 - 91)	1625
Fiat Uno (83 - 95)	0923
Fiat X1/9 (74 - 89)	0273
Ford Anglia (59 - 68)	0001
Ford Capri II (& III) 1.6 & 2.0 (74 - 87)	0283
Ford Capri II (& III) 2.8 & 3.0 (74 - 87)	1309
Ford Cortina Mk III 1300 & 1600 (70 - 76)	0070
Ford Cortina Mk IV (& V) 1.6 & 2.0 (76 - 83)	0343
Ford Cortina Mk IV (& V) 2.3 V6 (77 - 83)	0426
Ford Escort Mk I 1100 & 1300 (68 - 74)	0171
Ford Escort Mk I Mexico, RS 1600 & RS 2000 (70 - 74)	0139
Ford Escort Mk II Mexico, RS 1800 & RS 2000 (75 - 80)	0735
Ford Escort (75 - Aug 80)	0280
Ford Escort (Sept 80 - Sept 90)	0686
Ford Escort & Orion (Sept 90 - 00)	1737
Ford Fiesta (76 - Aug 83)	0334
Ford Fiesta (Aug 83 - Feb 89)	1030
Ford Fiesta (Feb 89 - Oct 95)	1595
Ford Fiesta (Oct 95 - 01)	3397
Ford Focus (98 - 01)	3759
Ford Granada (Sept 77 - Feb 85)	0481
Ford Granada & Scorpio (Mar 85 - 94)	1245
Ford Ka (96 - 99)	3570
Ford Mondeo Petrol (93 - 99)	1923
Ford Mondeo Diesel (93 - 96)	3465
Ford Orion (83 - Sept 90)	1009
Ford Sierra 4 cyl. (82 - 93)	0903
Ford Sierra V6 (82 - 91)	0904
Ford Transit Petrol (Mk 2) (78 - Jan 86)	0719
Ford Transit Petrol (Mk 3) (Feb 86 - 89)	1468
Ford Transit Diesel (Feb 86 - 99)	3019
Ford 1.6 & 1.8 litre Diesel Engine (84 - 96)	1172
Ford 2.1, 2.3 & 2.5 litre Diesel Engine (77 - 90)	1606
Freight Rover Sherpa (74 - 87)	0463
Hillman Avenger (70 - 82)	0037
Hillman Imp (63 - 76)	0022
Honda Accord (76 - Feb 84)	0351
Honda Civic (Feb 84 - Oct 87)	1226
Honda Civic (Nov 91 - 96)	3199
Hyundai Pony (85 - 94)	3398
Jaguar E Type (61 - 72)	0140
Jaguar MkI & II, 240 & 340 (55 - 69)	0098
Jaguar XJ6, XJ & Sovereign; Daimler Sovereign (68 - Oct 86)	0242
Jaguar XJ6 & Sovereign (Oct 86 - Sept 94)	3261
Jaguar XJ12, XJS & Sovereign; Daimler Double Six (72 - 88)	0478
Jeep Cherokee Petrol (93 - 96)	1943
Lada 1200, 1300, 1500 & 1600 (74 - 91)	0413
Lada Samara (87 - 91)	1610
Land Rover 90, 110 & Defender Diesel (83 - 95)	3017
Land Rover Discovery Petrol & Diesel (89 - 98)	3016
Land Rover Series IIA & III Diesel (58 - 85)	0529
Land Rover Series II, IIA & III Petrol (58 - 85)	0314
Mazda 323 (Mar 81 - Oct 89)	1608
Mazda 323 (Oct 89 - 98)	3455
Mazda 626 (May 83 - Sept 87)	0929
Mazda B-1600, B-1800 & B-2000 Pick-up (72 - 88)	0267
Mazda RX-7 (79 - 85)	0460
Mercedes-Benz 190, 190E & 190D Petrol & Diesel (83 - 93)	3450
Mercedes-Benz 200, 240, 300 Diesel (Oct 76 - 85)	1114
Mercedes-Benz 250 & 280 (68 - 72)	0346
Mercedes-Benz 250 & 280 (123 Series) (Oct 76 - 84)	0677
Mercedes-Benz 124 Series (85 - Aug 93)	3253
Mercedes-Benz C-Class Petrol & Diesel (93 - Aug 00)	3511
MGA (55 - 62)	0475
MGB (62 - 80)	0111
MG Midget & AH Sprite (58 - 80)	0265
Mini (59 - 69)	0527
Mini (69 - Oct 96)	0646
Mitsubishi Shogun & L200 Pick-Ups (83 - 94)	1944
Morris Ital 1.3 (80 - 84)	0705
Morris Minor 1000 (56 - 71)	0024
Nissan Bluebird (May 84 - Mar 86)	1223
Nissan Bluebird (Mar 86 - 90)	1473
Nissan Cherry (Sept 82 - 86)	1031
Nissan Micra (83 - Jan 93)	0931
Nissan Micra (93 - 99)	3254
Nissan Primera (90 - Aug 99)	1851
Nissan Stanza (82 - 86)	0824
Nissan Sunny (May 82 - Oct 86)	0895
Nissan Sunny (Oct 86 - Mar 91)	1378
Nissan Sunny (Apr 91 - 95)	3219
Opel Ascona & Manta (B Series) (Sept 75 - 88)	0316
Opel Kadett (Nov 79 - Oct 84)	0634
Opel Rekord (Feb 78 - Oct 86)	0543
Peugeot 106 Petrol & Diesel (91 - 01)	1882
Peugeot 205 Petrol (83 - 97)	0932
Peugeot 206 Petrol and Diesel (98 - 01)	3757
Peugeot 305 (78 - 89)	0538
Peugeot 306 Petrol & Diesel (93 - 99)	3073
Peugeot 309 (86 - 93)	1266
Peugeot 405 Petrol (88 - 97)	1559
Peugeot 405 Diesel (88 - 97)	3198
Peugeot 406 Petrol & Diesel (96 - 97)	3394
Peugeot 505 (79 - 89)	0762
Peugeot 1.7/1.8 & 1.9 litre Diesel Engine (82 - 96)	0950
Peugeot 2.0, 2.1, 2.3 & 2.5 litre Diesel Engines (74 - 90)	1607
Porsche 911 (65 - 85)	0264
Porsche 924 & 924 Turbo (76 - 85)	0397
Proton (89 - 97)	3255
Range Rover V8 (70 - Oct 92)	0606
Reliant Robin & Kitten (73 - 83)	0436
Renault 4 (61 - 86)	0072
Renault 5 (Feb 85 - 96)	1219
Renault 9 & 11 (82 - 89)	0822
Renault 18 (79 - 86)	0598
Renault 19 Petrol (89 - 94)	1646
Renault 19 Diesel (89 - 95)	1946
Renault 21 (86 - 94)	1397
Renault 25 (84 - 92)	1228
Renault Clio Petrol (91 - May 98)	1853
Renault Clio Diesel (91 - June 96)	3031
Renault Clio Petrol & Diesel (May 98 - May 01)	3906
Renault Espace Petrol & Diesel (85 - 96)	3197
Renault Fuego (80 - 86)	0764
Renault Laguna Petrol & Diesel (94 - 00)	3252
Renault Mégane & Scénic Petrol & Diesel (96 - 98)	3395
Rover 213 & 216 (84 - 89)	1116
Rover 214 & 414 (89 - 96)	1689
Rover 216 & 416 (89 - 96)	1830
Rover 211, 214, 216, 218 & 220 Petrol & Diesel (Dec 95 - 98)	3399
Rover 414, 416 & 420 Petrol & Diesel (May 95 - 98)	3453
Rover 618, 620 & 623 (93 - 97)	3257
Rover 820, 825 & 827 (86 - 95)	1380
Rover 3500 (76 - 87)	0365
Rover Metro, 111 & 114 (May 90 - 98)	1711
Saab 90, 99 & 900 (79 - Oct 93)	0765
Saab 95 & 96 (66 - 76)	0198
Saab 99 (69 - 79)	0247
Saab 900 (Oct 93 - 98)	3512
Saab 9000 (4-cyl) (85 - 98)	1686
Seat Ibiza & Cordoba Petrol & Diesel (Oct 93 - Oct 99)	3571
Seat Ibiza & Malaga (85 - 92)	1609
Skoda Estelle (77 - 89)	0604
Skoda Favorit (89 - 96)	1801
Skoda Felicia Petrol & Diesel (95 - 99)	3505
Subaru 1600 & 1800 (Nov 79 - 90)	0995
Sunbeam Alpine, Rapier & H120 (67 - 76)	0051
Suzuki Supercarry (86 - Oct 94)	3015
Suzuki SJ Series, Samurai & Vitara (4-cyl) (82 - 97)	1942
Talbot Alpine, Solara, Minx & Rapier (75 - 86)	0337
Talbot Horizon (78 - 86)	0473
Talbot Samba (82 - 86)	0823
Toyota Carina E (May 92 - 97)	3256
Toyota Corolla (Sept 83 - Sept 87)	1024
Toyota Corolla (80 - 85)	0683
Toyota Corolla (Sept 87 - Aug 92)	1683
Toyota Corolla (Aug 92 - 97)	3259
Toyota Hi-Ace & Hi-Lux (69 - Oct 83)	0304
Triumph Acclaim (81 - 84)	0792
Triumph GT6 & Vitesse (62 - 74)	0112
Triumph Herald (59 - 71)	0010
Triumph Spitfire (62 - 81)	0113
Triumph Stag (70 - 78)	0441
Triumph TR2, 3, 3A, 4 & 4A (52 - 67)	0028
Triumph TR5 & 6 (67 - 75)	0031
Triumph TR7 (75 - 82)	0322
Vauxhall Astra (80 - Oct 84)	0635
Vauxhall Astra & Belmont (Oct 84 - Oct 91)	1136
Vauxhall Astra (Oct 91 - Feb 98)	1832
Vauxhall/Opel Astra & Zafira Diesel (Feb 98 - Sept 00)	3797
Vauxhall/Opel Astra & Zafira Petrol (Feb 98 - Sept 00)	3758
Vauxhall/Opel Calibra (90 - 98)	3502
Vauxhall Carlton (Oct 78 - Oct 86)	0480
Vauxhall Carlton & Senator (Nov 86 - 94)	1469
Vauxhall Cavalier 1300 (77 - July 81)	0461
Vauxhall Cavalier 1600, 1900 & 2000 (75 - July 81)	0315
Vauxhall Cavalier (81 - Oct 88)	0812
Vauxhall Cavalier (Oct 88 - 95)	1570
Vauxhall Chevette (75 - 84)	0285
Vauxhall Corsa (Mar 93 - 97)	1985
Vauxhall/Opel Frontera Petrol & Diesel (91 - Sept 98)	3454
Vauxhall Nova (83 - 93)	0909
Vauxhall/Opel Omega (94 - 99)	3510
Vauxhall Vectra Petrol & Diesel (95 - 98)	3396
Vauxhall/Opel 1.5, 1.6 & 1.7 litre Diesel Engine (82 - 96)	1222
Volkswagen 411 & 412 (68 - 75)	0091
Volkswagen Beetle 1200 (54 - 77)	0036
Volkswagen Beetle 1300 & 1500 (65 - 75)	0039
Volkswagen Beetle 1302 & 1302S (70 - 72)	0110
Volkswagen Beetle 1303, 1303S & GT (72 - 75)	0159
Volkswagen Beetle (Apr 99 - 01)	3798
Volkswagen Golf & Jetta Mk 1 1.1 & 1.3 (74 - 84)	0716
Volkswagen Golf, Jetta & Scirocco Mk 1 1.5, 1.6 & 1.8 (74 - 84)	0726
Volkswagen Golf & Jetta Mk 1 Diesel (78 - 84)	0451
Volkswagen Golf & Jetta Mk 2 (Mar 84 - Feb 92)	1081
Volkswagen Golf & Vento Petrol & Diesel (Feb 92 - 96)	3097
Volkswagen Golf & Bora Petrol & Diesel (April 98 - 00)	3727
Volkswagen LT vans & light trucks (76 - 87)	0637
Volkswagen Passat & Santana (Sept 81 - May 88)	0814
Volkswagen Passat Petrol & Diesel (May 88 - 96)	3498
Volkswagen Polo & Derby (76 - Jan 82)	0335
Volkswagen Polo (82 - Oct 90)	0813
Volkswagen Polo (Nov 90 - Aug 94)	3245
Volkswagen Polo Hatchback Petrol & Petrol (94 - 99)	3500
Volkswagen Scirocco (82 - 90)	1224
Volkswagen Transporter 1600 (68 - 79)	0082
Volkswagen Transporter 1700, 1800 & 2000 (72 - 79)	0226
Volkswagen Transporter (air-cooled) (79 - 82)	0638
Volkswagen Transporter (water-cooled) (82 - 90)	3452
Volkswagen Type 3 (63 - 73)	0084
Volvo 120 & 130 Series (& P1800)(61 - 73)	0203
Volvo 142, 144 & 145 (66 - 74)	0129
Volvo 240 Series (74 - 93)	0270
Volvo 262, 264 & 260/265 (75 - 85)	0400
Volvo 340, 343, 345 & 360 (76 - 91)	0715
Volvo 440, 460 & 480 (87 - 97)	1691
Volvo 740 & 760 (82 - 91)	1258
Volvo 850 (92 - 96)	3260
Volvo 940 (90 - 96)	3249
Volvo S40 & V40 (96 - 99)	3569
Volvo S70, V70 & C70 (96 - 99)	3573